PRAY

HEAL

SLAY

The Millennial Woman's Guide for
Mind Renewal Through Faith After Failure

Linda Boateng

Disclaimer:

All biblical verses are extracted from the New Living Translation and the Good News Bible

First Printing, 2016
ISBN: 978-0-9975606-3-3

Cover and interior design by Vanessa Mendozzi
Images used under licence "Shutterstock.com"

CONTENTS

"Run your best in the race of faith, and win eternal life for yourself; for it was this that God called you when you firmly professed your faith before many witness" 1 Timothy 6:12

"He heals the broken hearted and bandages their wounds" (Psalm 147:3).

ACKNOWLEDGMENTS

God be the glory. I thank God for His guidance and authority in my life.

To my family. I love you for who you are, and I am thankful for your love, courage, and sacrifice. You gave up so much for me and I am forever indebted to you. I thank God for putting all of you in my life.

To my Bishop, counselor, and spiritual father: Thank you for uplifting me and helping me grow spiritually.

To my support system who consist of friends and mentors: Thank you for being a part of my life and encouraging me with your prayers, love and patience, I am truly grateful to have you in my corner.

CHAPTER 1:
A Love Letter to the Millennial Woman

Dear Millennial Woman, Insert your name here in the blank:

"My name is _____, I am clothed with strength and dignity, and I laugh without fear of the future. When I speak, my words are wise, and I give instructions with kindness." Proverbs 31:25-26

Do these words resonate with you? If so, I am happy to applaud you for embracing the comfort of the Scriptures. If not, I invite you to delve into this book on a journey with me. This book will open your eyes to the reality—you are loved and beautiful in every way through Christ. A reminder that you are strong and will be victorious. God loves your "flaws."

This is an inspirational Christian book for you, the Millennial woman. It's a simple but powerful message, from a young woman like you. She was painfully torn between pursuing a thriving career and cultural and societal pressure to start a family. Adding another level of stress was the fact that her biological clock was ticking loudly and was closing in on her. This is her message to all those young women:

- who struggle to find their identity in the face of societal pressures,
- and feels unworthy of love because her heart has been broken too many times
- who seems stuck in an unfulfilling relationship for too long;
- who lacks passion, purpose and is in search of belonging and validation;
- who is depressed and on the verge of defeat from life's disappointments;
- who puts pressure on herself to become someone she is not, because she compares herself to others and finds herself inadequate;
- who thinks she will always be a failure in life;
- who feels the pressure to become a wife and a mother before the age of 30;
- who married young and now has a need to find purpose or an identity;
- who had children at a young age and is in search of purpose
- who as a young mother, feels overwhelmed with the burden of motherhood
- who thinks no man will marry her because she had children out of wedlock;

... to all of these dear women, not only will you survive, you will change lives!

I hope this book inspires and shows you that victory *is* possible when you seek your identity in Christ and align yourself with His love and purpose, instead of giving in to the pressures of society that weigh so heavily on us. There are reflection questions at the end of some chapters to help you examine how you've lived your life. I hope you will take the message of this book to heart. Forgive yourself, surrender to God for healing, and seek to understand and—most importantly—renew your mind. Allow God to lead and reveal his purpose for your life. Then you will see yourself as a reflection of God's love. When you do, your life will change forever!

CHAPTER 2:
How did I get here?

So how did I get here? How did I get to this point where I am writing this book to share my testimony and show you the means to fight the hard battles of your life? I've arrived here—and am still journeying on—only after many setbacks and heartaches. As is the case with many things in life, this business of "let go and let God" is much easier said than done. And I didn't learn to rely on God until after some difficult experiences.

Your time will come

This is my story. In my early, twenties, I was obsessed with planning my life and setting goals at every stage of my life: I had to land my dream job by age 25, get married by 27, and have the first child by 28—all the while building a solid foundation for my career. According to my master plan, by age 40 I would be happily sharing my life with a loving family, enjoying the fruits of my hard work, and traveling—all on schedule. I expected God to help and support my plans. I chose when and how things would happen. Sounds Familiar?

Life looked at me and laughed at my arrogance. Before I knew it, I was 27 neither a wife nor a mother. I panicked. "What now? What have I done with my life?" It would seem to an outsider what I had accomplished thus far surpassed some people my age, but I something was missing. My progression the personal sense for me lacked substance, for years I thought, my happiness would come from marriage and kids. I was plagued by doubt and fear. I repeated the cycle of self pity like some millennial women do when disappointed by comparison and measuring the glass have empty. Without the constant agreement of the mind and the heart on God, there was room for confusion. Room for society to shape this millennial into a life of confusion and mediocrity.

The two paths of LIFE

*Are you living **LIFE** or being out lived by **life**?*

"It is better to take refuge in the Lord than to trust in people" (Psalms 118:8)

Dear Millennial woman, I'm here to tell you there are two paths of LIFE that shape your environment. The path based on confusion revolves around lethargy, ignorance, fear and ego. In the carnal world, know as living in the flesh where there is constant chaos and competition. Living in this world will have you tossed back and from life serving and living in your feelings. This is how the societal shapes your life. The carnal world operates in a state of fear, competition, comparison and judgment. As a millennial woman, I never felt fulfilled, because I craved instant gratification and selected experiences. I wanted to stay in control at all times as most millennial women do. Sometimes, the life you create in your mind is not what is dealt therefore, the frustration builds turning you to questioning God. When the mind and heart were never in agreement or aligned with God. Millennial woman, this lack of obedience will leave cracks for the enemy to cause havoc in your life.

On the other end of the scale of life is Love, Insight, Fearlessness, and Engagement/Egoless. The path to this stage requires a level of spiritual awareness and for me, that awareness came after countless failures, heartbreak and confusion. This stage requires the presence of GOD. Scenes from this realm began to emerge after I was baptized and started to truly experience the presence of God's guidance in my life. At times, my faith started to wavered and turned to God when I was in need but He never left me. As millennial women, at some point we craved a deeper closeness of unconditional love. That's what this path is about, total surrender to God. Operating in God's obedience. My surrender came after heartbreak and realizing my glass would never be half full without full submission to God. When I surrendered I found purpose in my pain.

What brought me to this point was a broken heart. The love I experience before surrendering was based on trusting man to reciprocate my feelings and each time that failed. As millennial women, it's is important to know there are lessons to be learned even from the smallest failures. After years of obsessing after what I thought was my ultimate purpose in life, I decided to break up with my old way of thinking and try living God's way. I wanted an identity my identity to sustain and direct me, so I reached out for the only power could trust, God.

Unfulfilled dreams and societal obsessions

What issues are you obsessing over in your life?

"That is why I tell you not to worry about everyday life—whether you have enough food and drink, or enough clothes to wear. Isn't life more than food, and your body more than clothing? Look at the birds. They don't plant or harvest or store food in barns, for your heavenly Father feeds them. And aren't you far more valuable to him than they are? Can all your worries add a single moment to your life?" Mathew 6:25-27

I encourage you to keep reading this passage to get a true scope of how incredible God's love is so you can stop worrying about your future. As millennial women, sometimes we allow heartbreaks and unfulfilled promises to deter us us from seeking purpose. Our failed attempts to plan life become obsessions as a result of trusting man. These obsessions can also be over unfulfilled timelines such as lack of marriage, kids, the dream career or pursing "The American Dream". Unresolved emotional issues can also cause you to descend into an endless hole of depression. Do not be disappointed over events you have no control over because God has already promised them to you. At some point in the millennial woman's life, there is a slight tendency to compare and allow societal standards to define you. Staying in this lane will hold you hostage and life will pass by. This causes a state of confusion, driven by fear and powered by jealousy, ego and Ignorance. I pray that you solidify your identity in Christ and seek understanding, purpose and love.

Your obsessions can lead to depression

Obsessing far too long can lead to hopelessness and depression. I fell into the trap of depression after my relationship ended, not only was I broken but all the other issues I failed to deal with compounded overtime from my past crept up on me. I was overwhelmed and internalizing every failure and rejection. I became so numb and hopeless, convinced God had forgotten about me. The numbness started wearing off, and I began to start feeling the pain and despair of my situation. I dwelt in this excruciatingly hopeless yearning for rescue yet the suffering did not ease. It felt like the nightmares I used to have in my childhood, where I fell from the top of a mountain and keep falling but never hit the ground. Fortunately, God intervened and I made a choice with all the energy I had to ask God to for healing—spiritually, mentally and physically. I had a long journey ahead but I had nothing to lose.

Healing

The first step of the healing process is asking God to help you understand why your situation is happening and to fill you with as much love as He can so you don't ever need validation from the carnal world. My dear millennial woman, my hope is that you feel God's love deeper than ever, and understand why He saved you for His purpose. God's love is the cure to mankind. We all want it so badly that we seek it out even from wrong people and in wrong places. Many people love based on mismatched soul ties, the bridge between two un-equally yoked people trying to make something out of their understanding of love. Healthy soul ties should be spiritually purpose driven. The point is no human can love you the way God loves you. Man's love only matters after you are grounded in God's love. Then, you seek a companion whose purpose aligns with yours to fulfill God's assignment.

Finding your root in God

"Yes, I am the vine; you are the branches. Those who remain in me and I in them will produce much fruit. For apart from me you can do nothing. And anyone who does not remain in me is thrown away like a useless branch and withers. Such branches are gathered into a pile to be burned." John 15:5-6 (NLT)

When a branch breaks from the vine it dries up and dies, in the same tone, any distractions from God when left unattended will cause destruction. The result of that is separation from the Fountain of Life, God Himself! It may be difficult to combat the negativity that the enemy tries hard to implant in our minds to distract us, but God did not give us the spirit of prayer and authority for nothing. He has given you the power to pray, heal and slay those fears and negative thoughts. So pour your heart out to God and watch Him move mountains in your life. With this testimony, I hope to draw you closer to God, and to show you how, God has the power to change your circumstance and empower you to emerge victorious from that situation. So what if that man left you with a broken heart? Let him go. So what if the promotion you thought was meant for you went to an undeserving coworker? Let it go. So what if that student loan or mortgage loan fell through? Let it go. You know why? You can let go because God is in control, and He is the only one who can give us ultimate happiness.

Yes, life throws will throw you many obstacles that show no mercy, but you *can* push through and win—by being rooted in God. Do not allow your situation to break you, make the choice to fight through the storm and speak faith into your life. You have a choice to speak the power of Faith or defeat in our life. It is that simple. Otherwise, when you give in to doubt and fear, you invite the enemy to further manipulate your life and throw you off track. There's nothing that the enemy enjoys more than watching a fearful Christian woman trying and failing to maneuver through life's trials. Trust that God is not a God of confusion. He didn't put you in a difficult situation just to confuse you. No, His plan for you is a future of hope and prosperity. So strengthen your faith—by praying, healing, and slaying your fears— and allow God to provide for all your needs and drive out the clouds of fear.

It is not my intent to preach or judge anyone on how they live their lives, but I would like my millennial sisters to know that straying from God's plan leads to the very problems that haunt and hinder our growth. Living life solely on your understanding (carnal teachings) is a dangerous way to live.

The cracks mean your love is out of order

God has to occupy your mind and heart in order for His will to manifest in your life. Hold on to this mantra while you're being tested. The true test comes from trusting God's timing and being patient. My "awakening" moment of insight emerged after rejection. Rejection from heartbreak will force you reflected on past setbacks and failures, which can steal your joy, opening a path for the enemy to sneak in and multiply the negative thoughts. Allowing those negative thoughts to fester will turn into a battle of the mind and heart. As soon as you notice the cracks, ask God for healing. Those areas not dedicated to God make your heart fertile soil for the devil to plant seed diving into a spiritual warfare. When this happens, it means your love is out of order. This occurs as you become captive to your feelings causing you to operated in the realm of carnality. You have to let God all the way in.

Trust and Surrender

"Lean on, trust and be confident in the Lord with all your heart and do not rely on your own sight or understanding" (Proverbs 3:5). As I learned to trust and have confidence in God, I went to Him and laid out before Him all my anger, rejection, depression, and desires, with an open mind and empty heart. I surrendered them to God, and prayed for healing.

Trust that if you are intent about walking and working for God, it will become apparent that His plans will manifest. You will also discover that He is very patient with us as He waits for the right time to carry out His plans. Patience is a hallmark of His love, and the purest form of love and is God's invitation to eternal peace. It makes sense that God abounds in patience just as His love overflows. As you continuously progress and model after God's love and patience, you'll learned so much about yourself. You see that without patience, you're easily frustrated and rush into making decisions without a clear vision. That is the reason most people struggle after a failure—rather than looking to God to lead and direct the path, there is a tendency to become impatient with God. Dear millennial woman, pray for the tools to make meaningful decisions, stop living in your feelings and allowing the Spirit make decisions for you. Don't neglect the basic principles that are key to joy.

"Before I was afflicted, I went astray, but now I keep your word." *Psalm 119:67(NKJV)*

"I used to wander off until you disciplined me; but now I closely follow your word." Psalms 119:67

As the psalmists expressed in these passages, to stray is human. It is not a struggle unique to you or me. But God is merciful and our ever present help. As He rescued me, so will He rescue you.

Surrendering to God for healing means allowing Him to penetrate your mind, body, and soul. The process of healing is gradual but in God you will encounter your ultimate purpose if you stay on course with prayer. Healing is a transformative that will vary per the individual. The process requires reconciling with God by giving up total control in order to walk in grace and favor. By letting go, you gain peace beyond understanding. These life lessons are worth the growing pains so seek Him out in prayer and see the transformation.

In order to heal, you have to reflect, regroup, and confront your past baggage. Trust me I know reaching back to some of those emotional issue can be terrifying. It may cause you to give up but instead trust the process and obey God's commands through prayer and stillness. God will stay by your side through the process and love you unconditionally through the pain and depression.

Stop running from pain

It is important to accept that no matter how much love you pour into someone, nothing is guaranteed to keep that person forever and God has a different plan for the people who exit our lives so keep living and chasing after God. Know that if your purpose partner's destiny was not aligned with yours, there was nothing anyone could do to keep them.

This realization taught me that the pain we experience in failure has a unique way of teaching us some of life's greatest lessons. Maybe pain in failure is telling you that whatever route you were on doesn't work, and you need to reroute. Maybe the reroute is where God intended us to play in the first place, you just failed to listen and comply. It is natural to want to avoid pain at all costs. I have tried it. As millennial women, we like to put on this armor of a tough exterior so we don't fall prey rejection or setbacks in life, but no matter how much we try to run from setbacks and pain, you are bound to come face to face with it at some point in life. So allow it to turn into a positive force. Listen to what pain is trying to tell you—it is time to make a change; it's time to move on; it's time to grow and heal through faith.

The pain from rejection has a way of making one vulnerable, even questioning your self-worth. However, it does not have to dominate your life. Rest assured that handing your pain and disappointments over to God brings peace. Allow God to work on your behalf with active prayer life. In doing so, you will exchange your burdens for the stillness of God's peace. Once you truly let go and experience God's peace over your life, your whole perspective on life positively changes. The refinement of confidence, boldness and authority become your sanity. It is a rebirth and everything in life starts making sense, your awareness is awakened, and every action or reaction line up with clarity.

As a millennial woman, you cannot allow setbacks in life debilitate you. Setbacks are reroutes to follow the right or a new path. It is ok to break up with old patterns that haven't worked before so you can reorder your according to God's plans. **Pain and suffering cannot shift your faith; they must increase your faith in those times.**

Pain has been a plague to the human race since the Garden of Eden, many of the unfortunate events that happened were turned around for good by God's good grace: Adam and Eve's disobedience, Cain and Abel's relationships with God, Jonah's escape from God's will, just to name a few examples. So trust that God's timing is perfect, and that all things work together for our good. God knows the appointed **Time, When, Where** and **Why** you only need to know the **How and what** to do to get His blessings. He knows every detail of your life—including the trials you are enduring—and understands your suffering. If you turn to Him and ask for help, He will lift you up and bless you with patience, love, and freedom to face adversity. Hold on to faith and persevere, as long as you hold on to God, He will guide and protect you.

Relying on God when you are in the throes of suffering does not mean you are expected to know how you will get through it. The how comes from commitment and asking the spirit for guidance. As you put one foot in front of the other, trusting God each step of the way, He will take care of the rest, while shielding you with strength unwavering love to help you through the process.

Whether you rush or delay the process of healing, in His perfect timing God will deliver and restore you for His purpose that suffering is never in vain. Whether the struggle is a lack of purpose, health issues, depression, rejection, loss of job, inability to conceive, or financial difficulties, whatever the situation maybe—none of these should define you. They may be the result of your disobedience to God, but in drawing near to Him, He will use these missteps to guide you in His direction. God has turned much evil into good throughout history, as the Bible tells us, and He can—and will—do the same with your missteps.

The struggles of depression and knowing when to get help

There are as many causes of heartache as there are people. What broke me is likely different from what breaks you down. Although we all have unique struggles, there is commonality in our suffering; fear, wavering faith or lack of faith. As I mentioned earlier, what caused my plunge into depression was a broken heart, failure to marry and have by a certain age of 30. After the milestone passed, I felt like I failed and became obsessive over this issue. I thought these were failures at the time due to my lack of knowledge of God. This arbitrary milestone was so important that I was certain that was my purpose in life and the beginning how God wanted me to live. When things did not go as perceived, I panicked and became utterly lost. By insisting on being the pilot of my life, rather than let the real Captain take control, I plunged into the ocean of depression.

That is my story. Yours might be similar or not but even as our complex stories crisscross in this web of life, this much is a reality: Millennial women are faced with so many issues that are the root cause of depression. Unfortunately, there is a negative stereotype over depressive issues in the many communities go ignored or silenced. Some pretend no one really suffers from depression. Others believe depression is a spirit that can be prayed away, because it is the devil's way of distracting us. This is true but sometimes it takes more than praying it away alone. The enemy knows and will use outside temptation from our purpose by plaguing us with depression, illnesses and confusion. In a context where the serious issues of depression are ignored, many believe seeking professional help or spiritual counseling is a sign of weakness and lack of faith. That is ridiculous, it is rather a strength of knowing and admitting you need help, is a sign you will survive and be victorious in this battle.

Contrary to what many may think, it takes courage to seek help. When you seek help, you bravely let in another person into our vulnerable life and humbly acknowledge our limitations—you cannot be in the right frame of mind to help ourselves when you are weighed down and crushed by hopelessness and defeat. In my situation I didn't realize how deep I had drifted away until the eleventh hour, although I was fasting and praying, I needed additional help to emerge from the darkness that shrouded me for months. In spiritual counseling, I learned something I could not see on my own: the devil is limited by time. It is true that if you give him an inch, he will work overtime to turn you against yourself, convince you there is no hope, and harp on you the message that you are unworthy of love or not needed in this world. But his influence only lasts for a moment and is no comparison to the dominion of the omnipotent God over my mind and my life. The enemy is no threat to God's sovereignty.

God has always had a different plan for me and it took me a while to hear His voice but now it is clear. After fighting it for so long and realizing what I was doing was not working, I retreated and gave up all control to Jesus. It became clear that life boils down to two choices, the flesh that thrives on instant gratification or the peace that comes only from a genuine relationship with reliance on God. When you single-mindedly pursue your own plans, your success or failure to achieve those plans becomes pressure points that the enemy uses to distract you from the quest to obtain God's grace and mercy. But we can be spared so much pain and depression when we entrust our life to God and allow Him to build up our inner core. The inner core is where the spirit dwells, and when it is strong, it shows God's true intentions for us. When we begin to reflect God's love and peace from our inner core, there is a rebirth and the future has endless possibilities. Trust me, no man has ever won a victory while dwelling in the flesh.

"No, dear brothers and sisters, I have not achieved it but I focus on this one thing: Forgetting the past and looking forward to what lies ahead, I press on to reach the end of the race and receive the heavenly prize for which God, through Christ Jesus, is calling us." Philippians 3:13-14

Let's heed Paul's counsel here, to forget the past and look forward. We can learn from the past and then let it go, by accepting God's help. The lessons learned will help us develop a stable and mature character. In this process, your personal relationship with God has to be the center of your existence.

CHAPTER 3

Societal pressures on the millennial woman

The plague of societal pressures

What are some societal pressures you need to break away from your life?

I can think of many I had to demolish. Since the majority of our society do not use the Bible as the standard and guide for living, and few acknowledge Jesus as their Lord and Savior, it is no surprise that those who *are* Christians are bombarded with values that run contrary to their belief. In every aspect of life, the millennial woman is bound to face pressure from the society to conform to worldly standards. The world gives a different set of expectations from what the Bible teaches us: how we understand beauty, virtue, morality, success, etc. Each of these things merits a book on its own, but in this chapter I want to focus some of the pressures single

Millennial women face and the expectation that we must hit major milestones in life on a preset schedule.

Media Influence

The media communicates to us what the society considers acceptable. Everywhere in the media it is clear what this carnal world's rules and ideals are regarding how the Millennial woman should live or look. These worldly standards create a conflict between our flesh and spirit, keeping them in a perpetual tug-of-war. The Millennial woman will become overwhelmed all too soon, if she does not have a firm identity in Christ. Without security in Christ we will spend the majority of our life coveting. Some conform with societies ideologies, regretting the past and rushing into hasty decisions that may result in long-lasting consequences. Therefore, it is paramount that you have God on your side as you fight against the tide of our society and the pressure it puts on you.

When your focus shifts away from conforming to the society and turns to God's purpose for your life, it is much easier to resist the enemies tricks. The devil even uses the people closest to you to lure you away from God. So we must be vigilant and guard our heart and mind against negativity and temptations. These temptations can come in all shapes and forms. We may be tempted to feel depressed that you do not measure up to the society's standards, you may be tempted to compare ourselves to others, we may be tempted to give in to fear that we are not good enough. Slay all these temptations!

Slay the society's expectations of the Millennial woman! As soon as you are in Christ, you are a new creation. Your past is dead and gone. The society has no claim on you, so do not waste your time trying to please the society. Instead, strive to act as a reflection of Jesus. Continue to be a work in progress for God's army. Work, walk and worship as such.

When people accuse you of acting false and remind you of your past, explain that the past is, well, the *past*, and it qualifies you as someone who has overcome the past to share your testimony. Do not allow other people or the devil to hold you captive in your past. Your past has been forgiven and you have been redeemed by God himself.

The biological clock

For some reason, many millennial women want to follow a certain time line to get married, have kids, car, dog and nice home, all by age 30. Why? It's as if we are damaged goods after you turn 30 years old. This absurd pressure from the society needs to be burnt at the root. It puts all of us women into a rigid box, assuming that we are factory-made robots that mechanically go through life without ever encountering unavoidable setbacks or life changes. It assumes that all that there is to a woman's life is attending college, landing a good internship after graduating from college (with a mountain of student loans that keep her trapped for eternity), and getting a job in her trained field—and during this process finding a husband and becoming a mother. Yes, all of these things are important, but a woman is so much more than the combination of these milestones! In my African culture, it appears the only acceptable careers are in medicine, law, science, or engineering. Once a person has secured training and a job in one of those fields, the next step is getting married, having kids, and living happily ever after—again, on a strict time line of accomplishing it all by age 30.

Society wants the millennial woman to believe that women begin wasting away after a certain age, and design her to control her life and trust man. This state of ignorance causes the millennial woman to be in a constant battle of an identity crisis. The caged box where you make decisions based on feelings and become a slave to them. It limits the millennial woman who wants to find life's meaning. Seeking an identity in Christ does not have a time line or expiration date. Society has a way of making the millennial woman feel incomplete when she's not married with children by age 30. No of this matters when you find your identity in Christ.

The identity of the millennial woman

Are you living on societal pressures or biblical teachings?

For a while, I honestly thought my ultimate purpose was to be married and have children as expected in many cultures. I think being a wife and a mother is one of the highest blessings in life, but it should not be our ultimate goal. Our identity is first a child of Christ, and anything else comes only second to that. The danger and irony of fitting women into a box is vividly captured in the lyrics below. Ironically, there is a Beyoncé song called "Flawless," which features a cameo by Chimamanda Ngozi Adichie a Nigerian novelist and educator. Women are in many ways taught to be in the background and not be the overachiever because it devalues the man. Society and some cultures teach girls not to be as ambitious or career oriented, instead girls should limit their goals to being housewives or anything other than making the man feel 'powerless'. Young women are told that marriage, having children is the source of happiness and so marriage becomes the young woman's ultimate goal in life. Instead of empowering them to dream bigger and providing them with tools and resources and education to achieve those aspirations. It is a fact that society tries to pin women against each other by comparing their physical attributes like weight, skin color, yet for the man the competition is based on their profession, strength and heavy bank accounts.

False expectations of the Ultimate Goal

Millennial women who find their identity in Christ are defying all odds, living purposeful lives, and making sure whomever the man God is readying for them as their partners is purposefully aligned with them for Gods glory.

Do not get me wrong—We still want to have a husband and children, but that is not the millennial woman's ultimate goal and destiny but as gifts already promised by God, and in His time. The ultimate purpose in life is fulfilling your assignment, and sometimes it takes a lifetime to discover your purpose. Knowing your identity in Christ leads to finding purpose. When you know the purpose of your life, you can run full it in pursuit of that purpose, without comparing yourself to others, without regretting the past. Moreover, life will be full of possibilities!

The level of false expectations placed on young women by society sets them up to fail, physically, spiritually, and mentally. To combat the false expectations of society, it is crucial that you spend time listening to God in solitude. In the stillness of those moments, listen to what God has to say about who you are and why He intricately formed you. We cannot cultivate a sensitivity to God's voice if we allow the noises of the world to drown us. As a result, we rob ourselves of the opportunity to know the truth when we hide behind societies ideologies rather than building genuine relationships, fellowshipping and blessing others with our gifts. We spend so much time on social media that we become more obsessed about maintaining an image on those sites rather than tending to our duties as servants of Christ. Not tending to our mental, physical and spiritual well-being, so many people are consumed with what others are portraying on Snapchat, Instagram and Facebook they forget they were created for a purpose not to people watch. Some millennial women forget about life, and as a result, the enemy sucks life out of them. It is time that we recognize the need to turn away from social media, and toward spending time with God and edifying others.

Societal ideologies along with inconsistent cultural and traditional norms tend to drown out the voice of

God and lead into temptation. Social media has taken over as primary communication tool, and it is a great tool for businesses, and spreading news. Although social media has helped our world in many ways, it has also opened Pandora's Box and unleashed various of temptations and traps more than ever, such as luring millennial women to compare themselves to the Joneses, seek instant gratification and the urge to accumulate riches we cannot take to the grave. Some millennial women get lost in virtual reality, abandoning their God given identity.

When you become a captive to society's false expectations, and abandon your identity in Christ, you undervalue true potential. Nothing compares even remotely to the gifts awaiting you, and you can have it all through Christ. I want to help the millennial woman understand, you can have it all, if you focus on God. Your obedience is key and also a choice. Do not undervalue your gifts or feel you are delayed in life, because you are in your 20's, 30's or 40's and still not married and nowhere near achieving your plans. God is preparing you in His presence without undervaluing His purpose for your life, and you will be blessed with your purposeful husband, so that you can live out your testimony and walk in grace. This by no means an empty reassurance from me but a solid promise from the Creator of the world to you, as this verse reminds us:

"And this same God who takes care of me will supply all your needs from his glorious riches which have been given to us in Christ Jesus." Philippians 4:19

Having it all begins with contentment and seeking your identity in God is the only way to live out a purposeful life. Whether in your season of singleness or as a single mother, Paul encouraged single Christians to work for the Lord. While you are waiting for God to bless you with marriage and children, be patient and work for God. In Corinthians, Paul proclaims:

"I want you to be free from the concerns of this life. An unmarried man can spend his time doing the Lord's work and thinking how to please Him. But a married man has to think about his earthly responsibilities and how to please his wife. His interests are divided. In the same way, a woman who is no longer or has never been married can be devoted to the Lord and holy in body and in spirit. But a married woman has to think about her earthly responsibilities and how to please her husband. I am saying this for your benefit, not to place restrictions on you. I want you to do whatever will help you serve the Lord best, with as few distractions as possible." 1 Corinthians 7:32-35

The carnal world wants women to feel as though being single and virtuous is a curse. It is definitely not, singleness can produce a stillness where God will reveal your calling and identity. Blind pursuit of marriage and motherhood will give us no solid self-identity. Do not believe the society when it tells you the ultimate goal of your existence is to get married and keep up with the Joneses. No, the ultimate goal for Christians is to fulfill God's purpose for us.

"As Isaiah said, 'Rejoice, O Childless woman, you who have never given birth! Break into a joyful shout, you who have never been in labor! For the desolate woman now has more children than the woman who lives with her husband." Galatians 4:27

This verse shows us that throughout history, there were many desolate woman unable to have children but their faith changed everything. It shows us God knows the pain of being without a child. Like Hannah's story, when her husband's second wife had children before she did, Hannah cried out to God, and while in her time of patiently waiting, she praised and was obedient. As a result, the Lord blessed her with many children. Her story is such a blessing to me, no matter my circumstance.

False Confidence without God

"But if you remain in me and my words remain in you, you may ask for anything you want, and it will be granted." John 15:7

Despite the abundant blessings available in Christ, in my 20's as a millennial woman, I was distracted from pursuing God. Instead, my sole focus was pursuing a successful career and financial independence much like other millennial women. Due to the vernal success and independence (having a paying job, buying material objects and not having to struggle for much), but it was an empty confidence, gained from societal ideologies. Any confidence gained outside of Christ can only be shaky at best. My "independence" without dependence on God was dangerous, as it drew me further away from my true provider. My mind occasionally pondered on God but not fully engaged. My fellow millennial women do not believe the world when it tells you that you should depend on your own wisdom and instinct. The more you depend on yourself, the less you will consult God for your decisions. But why would we rob ourselves of the infinite wisdom of God? Let us all strive to depend on God more than on ourselves!

As a twenty something year old, I involuntarily strayed from God before learning the sweetness of depending on Him. Prior to surrendering, I not only planned my life, I also compiled an inventory of qualities I wanted in a future husband. I had my long list of "must haves". Many millennial women have the same mindset to shoot for such a lofty ideal that we end up being unrealistic. At times we fail to conduct a self-evaluation to list the qualities we have to offer, we list demands for God in exchange for nothing, traits of a modern day Israelite. Let God perfect your qualities as a child of God and when you're ready he will bless you with a purpose partner.

Something about turning 30 that makes a woman reflect on life and ponder about her the future; this can be daunting at times without total faith in God. The truth is millennial woman, life does not *end* at 30 in fact it is the age of awakening. The age where you realize it is time to live with a purpose. There is no reason to despair if you reach age 30 and do not have it all together. There is nothing wrong with not having the traditional life by age 30 as long as you know your identity, purpose, and God's promise. Millennial woman should not be defined by societal standards or cultural norms.

Yes, some people may look down on you, questioning if something is wrong with you and why you're not married by 30. Cultural and societal spectators may interpret it as hidden weaknesses or assume you are incompetent without the "dream job". WRONG! You are not defined by human opinions. If you are solid in God's presence, no one can take his promises from you. God will bless you with all these things in His own good time. God's miracles are always on time! I have witnessed God's grace when a close friend of mine gave birth to her first child in her 40's, what a testament of God's faithfulness. If God is determined to bless you with something, nothing can stop Him—not even your biological clock!

Comparison steal your joy

Are you still comparing your life to others? STOP!

Romans 12:2 says, *"Do not copy the behavior and customs of this world, but let God transform you into a new person by changing the way you think. Then you will learn to know God's will for you, which is good and pleasing and perfect.*

My millennial woman, it is essential to focus less on the worldly voices and more on walking, worshiping and working for a purpose. As you patiently wait, stop comparing yourself with your peers, living in your feelings and stop believing the lies on social media. Do not rush into a relationship or pressure a man to marry you. From my experience, drift could drift away, ending the relationship abruptly and leaving your heart in tatters. How well I know that! Comparison kills your spirit, the thief of joy, and it causes us to forget that God is on a mission behind closed doors working on our behalf. You have your own life to live, you have unique gifts and a purpose to fulfill. Comparison creates an environment in which you neglect your own strengths, that is the enemy's tool. The result of it is covetousness, irrevocable decisions, depression, low self-esteem, and even worse, suicide. Comparison is a self-inflicted and painful disorder. You can choose to ignore the society's invitations of comparison and pursue God's unique goals for your life.

When you immerse yourself in God's will for your life, you will develop spiritually, mentally, physically and financially. You will gradually carve out the life God intended for you, and the sweetness and light of that success will overshadow what you once viewed as past failures. It will be a success that is distinctively your own. Psalms 46:10 says, *"Be still and know that I am God."* I love this verse because it reminds us that God reveals things to you when you are still and He breathes new life into you. You will never ever be the same after that stillness. So run away from the pressures of society, enter into this stillness with the Lord, and begin to focus on living a life designed for you.

This dependence and focus on God applies not only to single millennial women; it is just as relevant for everyone else. If you are blessed with a family yet feel, you are not living up to your potential due to lack of identity or purpose, intentionally find time for God to develop your gifts.

"They themselves will be wealthy, and their good deeds will last forever. Light shines in the darkness for the godly. They are generous, compassionate, and righteous." Psalms 112:3-4

The pressures millennial women constantly face from the society give us the false message that if you do not measure up, your life is not worth living. That's the enemies work at hand, in full force. However, as this passage from the Psalms tells us, light shines even in darkness. Let us hold fast to the message of light, and await God's plans to manifest rather than pursuing empty goals in darkness.

Living in your feelings disturb your peace

If you follow the voices of the society and find yourself in the throes of pain because you have not met the society's expectations, do not despair. Society bases every thought on feelings. Those feelings only draw you to react in ways that most times seem un-Christian like. Feelings disturb your peace. Anything that disturbs your peace is of God. When you choose to live in your feelings, you are controlling the space God should be occupying. God is greater than your feelings and you simply cannot live for God and your feelings. You have to choose one.

Going through life's trials can make you thirst for God's presence more than ever. This can be an opportunity for you to rebuild a robust relationship with God. However, when you are making your way back to God, be ready for fiery temptations because the devil wants to you stay in your pain. The devil will do everything possible to direct you away from the path of light and truth. Perhaps more than before, you will struggle with doubt and fear. The devil will make you question, "Well, if God is perfect and has good plans for me, then why would He watch me suffer?" The devil will throw at you all kinds of negative thoughts and feelings. But don't be deceived. Life is hard, and there are difficult questions to answer. God always tests your heart before giving you a lesson so pray and endure it. Be patient, lean on God, and trust Him to give you the answers you need. The devil will use all kinds of tricks to deter you from God, whether in relationships, jobs, or illnesses.

You have to be intentional in your process of healing from the past, and be ready to face your pain and suffering. When you are intentional about facing your pain, then healing will be our prize. When you're intentional with God, He'll be intentional about your prayers.

Don't give in to the enemies tricks

"This great dragon the ancient serpent called the devil, or Satan, the one deceiving the whole world was thrown down to the earth with all his angels." Revelations 12:9

"But I am not surprised! Even Satan disguises himself as an angel of light." 2 Corinthians 11:14

Another thing you must guard against in your process of healing is that the devil may come in the disguise of an angel of light. I mentioned before that he will trick us into questioning God, and drown us with negative thoughts. But the enemy may also trick us with positive things—he may deceive us into thinking that comparing ourselves to others can be good for us (it can motivate us to grow, can't it?), or that getting married and having children by 30 makes perfect sense (everyone else is doing it, why miss out?). No matter how packages his lies, the lies are lies. Focus on His word and trust that God will renew your mind according to His promises and give you peace, because you have grace on your side.

Grace gives us the armor to fight temptation. Grace is the reason Jesus gave up His life for us, and it gives us an open invitation to God's presence. Therefore, walking in grace takes reconciling with God, living, walking and worshiping him 24/7. The devil wants us to forget the grace given to us so that in order to loose hope. Remember, you are stronger than your struggle. The devil will try to consume your mind with negative thoughts and plans of demise. At all costs, try to find solace in God because a mind that wavers in faith will always struggle to entrust all to God, and that is exactly what the enemy wants. Believe, instead, that God does not change, so His favor upon you does not change and He *will* come through for you. He *is* greater than your pain. Take to heart this comforting promise in the Bible:

"For the Lord your God is living among you. He is a mighty savior. He will take delight in you with gladness. With his love, he will calm all your fears. He will rejoice over you with joyful songs." *Zephaniah 3:17*

CHAPTER 4:
Investing in your spirituality

"For I know the plans I have for you,' says the LORD. 'They are plans for good and not for disaster, to give you a future and a hope." Jeremaih 29:11

Besides societal pressure points, I had emotional pressure points from childhood issues I never dealt with, which rolled over into my relationships. We all have childhood issues that we forget about that surface in adulthood. Before we make sense of various things that have molded us, we sometimes foolishly run head-on into life, thinking we can control life and make plans without understanding who we really are. But remember, everything happens for a purpose, and God knows what that purpose is. So, rather than making your own plans according to your understanding, seek advice from the ultimate source. Life is a choice. You can choose to truly live or just exist. You can choose to stay enslaved to the society's unrealistic pressures, continue sulking in your resentment toward those who wronged you, or choose to shield with faith.

Confronting the Past and Forgiveness

If everything happens for a purpose, and if God has a plan for you, it makes more sense to face those past issues and ask God to heal you from them, rather than allowing them to hold you back until you explode. At some point as an adult we have to accept how our current circumstance but also realized how we were raised is a factor in our decision making. Those who raised us have a major role in how we relate to others. If what you are used to is not working, ask God to give you the courage to let it go. Old habits die slow so be patient with yourself. I once heard Mark Nepo in an interview say "Sacrifice is giving up what no longer works in order to stay close to what is sacred." I thought, "Wow! If only I knew this before, I would not have harbored so much anger growing up, and I could have enjoyed life a bit more." Thankfully, it is not too late.

Are there emotional issues for the past you need to confront?

God loves you enough to give you a second chance to help others by sharing your testimony. During the healing process, God may reveal some deep rooted issues buried so deep you'll be petrified at digging them up. You will feel exposed when those unexpected issues surface, but weathering the process of healing teaches forgiveness of others, and most importantly yourself. Sometimes it takes having a conversation with loved once who hurt us about how our past issues affect our currently. These conversations create an opportunity for growth, and it is your choice to heal from past emotional issues or let it keep festering. The struggle for forgiveness is a choice even after allowing God in. Confronting past emotional issues and people from our past is essential in spiritual growth. The past is a hostage time capsule that eventually erupts, but when you follow God's lead, He will enlighten you to break free from the chains holding you hostage.

Parental connections affect relationships in adulthood

In addition to my struggles with sustaining an emotional connection with others, I have had other problems that originated in my relationship with my father. When you live in an environment where people do not express emotions, it will naturally be hard for you to express emotions as an adult. In my healing, I learned that having an emotionally open and positive relationship with your parents paves the way for healthy relationships in adulthood. Interactions among the parents and their children will determine how you maintain and cultivate relationships. Dealing with my past emotional and childhood issues made me realize I can't close the door to the feelings of your temporary situation, because eventually, you will have to deal with them. You may unintentionally create emotional dumpsters by not dealing with past and current hurts. Do not shove them away. Shoving rejection, abandonment, betrayal away will eventually resurface. I know first hand it is easier the burry them than carry the burden. In many ways this is a coping mechanism due to lack of dependence on God. Allowing God to remain present in any situation brings a just outcome. Not confronting or resolving those emotional issues can deplete your energy and leave your love tank empty. As a result, you may transfer those feelings into future relationships causing unnecessary pain to others. This is why it is vital to let God handle your burdens in the heat of the moment and seek understanding or healing. In order for God to position you in the assigned territory, you have to heal from the scars because your next level will require a new lens.

Letting go of toxic people

Are you relationships approved by God?

After the most recent setback and depression, I had to go through a series of transformations, including restructuring how I related others, and these changes rebuilt me into a stronger person. I committed to prayer and allowed God to renew my mind, body, and spirit. It may seem difficult at times to continuously pray and not see instant changes but rest knowing that God is working behind the scenes. Prayer is good for the soul. Allow your brokenness to humble you and strengthen you to tackle life by its horns. The decisions you make sometimes lead to our setbacks. Sometimes as millennial women, you make permanent decisions over temporary situations. Don't get caught up in your feelings that you shut our eyes to the red flags God tried to show you. It vital to ask God's approval when entering into any type of friendship. If a relationship lacks God's approval, it is bound to fail.

In order for any relationship to succeed, whether personal or business, you have to bring the relationship before God. Otherwise, when you try to steer these relationships according to our own plans and wisdom, you are surely inviting chaos and confusion into our life. Dear millennial woman, don't get so busy and make excuses to neglect communicating with God. Do not take God for granted, every breath you take is not by chance. He wakes us up each morning so that you can accomplish His purpose for our lives. As such, with every breath you must worship and praise Him, whether you're down or having the best day of your life. Honor God and bring every relationship before Him for His blessing and approval. We only get hurt because we trusted man to uphold their loyalty to us instead of waiting on God. Cease to take life into our own hands out of fear of the future. Stop rushing ahead of God when it comes to relationships.

Rejection, when it comes to your career, love or life in general makes you want to shut people out or refuse to give second chances. The pain may hold you back from allowing people in but think of how God so generously gives us a second change to live right each day. Pray that God gives you the strength to give people a chance to help you maneuver through life a little easier. Allow those who are wiser to drop some knowledge into you and feed you spiritually. Millennial woman, don't push those people away. Nurture and salvage those friendships that build your character and growth, do not fail to put in the effort out of fear of rejection or lack of trust. Let go of the people who disturb your peace it is ok to let go of loved once who don't have your best interest at heart. Don't hold on or recycle toxic relationships out of fear of

being alone. Pray for discernment and God will show
you who is in or out.

People and Timing

Are you holding on to people you need to get go?

It is important to recognize some connections with
people are timed, and should not last longer than they
should. It could be for years or mere minutes. Sometimes
people come into our lives for help, or to teach us a
lesson, but we end up letting them outstay their welcome
and they end up hurting us. We have to recognize when it
is time to let go and take accountability for our part in
the noise. But regardless of the length we are to make
peace and be gentle with each other. With the assistance
of the Spirit, we are to forgive and love one another, even
if from a distance.

*"It is full of mercy and the fruit of good deeds. It shows no
favoritism and is always sincere."* James 3:17

This verse brings me much comfort, and I hope it
comforts you, too. All of us have made mistakes that we
beat ourselves up for, and there are times when we dig
ourselves into a situation beyond salvage. You might
question God's authority and goodness, or believe you
are being punished. But this verse—and countless other
verses—reminds us God is full of mercy.

Your circumstance may seem bleak with nowhere to
turn or you may be stricken with fear of the unknown
with no rescue in sight—I know what that's like. God is

your rescue. Trust Him to relieve the pain and suffering, for He is a covenant-keeping God and will surely provide you with the peace only He can supply. Whatever suffering you find yourself in, with prayer there is redemption.

Remember that we're not created to fight and walk through life alone. God is our ever present help and He also sends messengers in disguise to share in our burdens. There's no cost to listening and doing it God's way. Do not try to force things to go your way because it will be only a cycle of disappointments and delays—I did it, and I lived in that cycle for months of darkness. In that darkness when there seemed to be no hope, God brought me to see a ray of hope—His own radiant promise. It does not take hitting rock bottom for you to say, "Yes, I'll do it your way." God has so many unopened promises in store for you. The moment you agree to God's plans, true freedom and liberation arise. Dear millennial woman, I hope that you, too, will give up fighting it all on your own and in prayer seek to understand God is faithful.

Contentment

Are you happy where you are in life?

I used to obsess over my own plans for life and I would pray for things to go as I had planned, it made sense at the time when instant gratification ruled my life. But one day it dawned on me that forcing things to happen only distances us from God's plan for us. By insisting on our desires, we create our own delays in life and cause our own unhappiness. Dear millennial woman, I know it may be tough at times to be happy in the storm but be thankful for the favor and grace God has already shown you. Be patient with your progress and with others as God continues to unfold His promises in your life. Contentment and joy are the result of knowing God's is intentional about his blessings for you and there is no need to waste time worrying about the future. So be at peace and keep praying, be grateful for your current circumstances and thank God for the small blessings.

Without cultivating an attitude of thanksgiving and contentment, you leave room for the enemy to deceive you. From experience, I know there can be a momentary solace in shifting the blame to God because it makes us feel better about a situation because honestly no one likes to be the cause of his or her own misfortunes. Remember that in God's presence lies perfect love and pure joy.

"Therefore, be careful to obey every command I am giving you today, so you may have strength to go in and take over the land you are about to enter." Deuteronomy 11:8

Sometimes we cause our own mistakes

Are you hindering your progress?

Admitting that you are the cause of your own problems is a tough pill to swallow especially when your decisions felt right at the time. Owning your mistake takes humility so remember that the rescue you need only God can provide. All your sins, guilt and shame, pride and wrongs—everything—have already been nailed to the cross and redeemed by Jesus. You don't need to carry those overweight burdens any longer. Embrace the gospel that Jesus has paid for your past *in full*. Lay down all your burdens at the feet of the cross in prayer, for that's where all your worries and debts end. Don't let your failures drive out your blessings. The blessings God has for you outweigh what you can buy yourself. There is a massive warehouse full of blessings with your name on them, and the only path to them is obedience to God. The call to obedience produces strength.

Enduring the storm through obedience

In what ways can you be more obedient?

Obedience gives us direction in life through the Holy Spirit who dwells within us. I call it your best friend, some may call the voice in our head—the good one or "instinct." It is important to take advantage of it to see God's vision for your life. When you adhere to God's guidance, you gain clarity in all circumstances. There will be no more confusion. The right time to humble yourself and practice obedience is now. Stay in obedience with prayer and move only when the Spirit nudges you. Remember the story of Paul's thorn in his flesh, a reminder that obedience takes patience and contentment. He cried out to God to remove the thorn from his flesh, but the Lord simply answered to his pleas with this reassurance: *"My grace is all you need, My power works best in your weakness" (2 Corinthians 12:9)*. When Paul finally understood God's will, he boasted about his pain because it was in his pain that the power of Christ would manifest and he would be strengthened. I'm not saying that you should announce to the world that you're in pain, but I encourage you to be patient and persevere as you wait for God to sustain and strengthen. When we're between seasons it is easier to focus on the storm than the harvest awaiting us. Use this process to find the source of the pain or failure and heal from it. Pray for wisdom and increased faith; pray that God provides wisdom and understanding in your circumstances. Lean on Him, and He will give you clarity and growth.

If you skip the process of enduring and learning from your pain, you will cheat yourself out of some of life's greatest lessons and end up recycling the same situations over again. While you're sulking in the pain and allowing the enemy to whisper negative thoughts to you, life is passing you by. Time waits for no man. It is your choice to let the enemy deceive you and stall your growth, or to let God be the captain of your life and lead you to victory.

The enemy awaits to devour you

"Stay alert! Watch out for your great enemy, the devil. He prowls around like a roaring lion, looking for someone to devour. Stand firm against him, and be strong in your faith. Remember that your family of believers all over the world is going through the same kind of suffering like you are. In His kindness, God called you to share in his eternal glory by means of Christ Jesus. So after you have suffered a little while, he will restore, support, and strengthen you, and he will place you on a firm foundation." 1 Peter 5:8-9

Dear millennial women, as you surrender control to God and allow Him to accomplish His plans for your life, the devil will be lurking at every corner, ready to pounce upon you with his tricks and lies. Be vigilant against deception. It's inevitable that you will have small setbacks in your walk with God, because we are all fallible, but God who has no beginning or end will always accept you anytime with open arms. If you stumble, pray for strength to subdue the distractions. No matter how bleak you think your situation is, God can change it around in a millisecond so stay committed in prayer. Trust Him to work miracles—that's His specialty and He's done it before and will surprise you each time. Cry out to God when things get tough. Praise Him especially in the bad times, and in all situations, be content and obedient. God will deliver you and perfect your life in due time.

CHAPTER 5:
Mental health and understanding depression

Reflect on your life for a moment

What issues cause you to fall into depression?

Worry, fear of loneliness, loss of a loved one or lack of finances, these are all issues that can cause one to lose hope and fall into a depression. Depression is a terrible disease that cause many to lose hope in their circumstance. Dear millennial women, I know you may need to retreat or even blame yourself for depressive state but know you are not alone many suffer from this illness. The feelings of defeat, rejection, hopelessness or feeling like you are unworthy of love are all tricks of the enemy to distract you from the bigger picture. They sometimes all surface at once, but know there is help. If you catch yourself consistently blaming yourself for your pain, beware that it may be a sign of depression.

Depression is a serious illness. It robs you of every ounce of sanity you may have left. The enemy uses depression to lure others by dragging them down or causing them to question God's goodness. Depression clouds the mind with thoughts and feelings of despair. Instead of denying or ignoring depression, we should be talking about it in our communities, churches, households and schools. Until we acknowledge and pay attention to it in open conversations, we cannot combat it through prayer and support systems alone. It's a silent epidemic, with countless people suffering from it behind closed doors. We will never know who is suffering if we continue to stigmatize it.

When society chooses to stigmatize or ignore depression, people who truly suffer from it are forced to put up a happy façade as they suffer inside. How many people's lives have fallen apart, and how many have been driven to suicide, because they cannot share their pain with others without risking being judged? If we are to be truly God's children who champion love and truth, we need to advocate for a greater awareness of depression and its effects on people and their families and friends.

Sometimes when we face death or failure, the load plummets into depression and profound self-blame. It is not just the heart that suffers, but it becomes ripple effect that touches every aspect of your life. In some instances, it can affect you physically, financially and mentally. It may seem like with every turn, life swallows you up and you become numb and emotionally handicapped. Every area of your life may seem like it is under attack so badly that it becomes difficult to know which problem to tackle first. The deeper you get the more some of those problems surface and all you want is for your heart to stop beating so the pain can vanish. Sadly, some even contemplate death thinking it is a far better solution than the misery they are experiencing. We have to unite as a community to open dialog on the topic of depression.

Fear can hold you hostage

Are you allowing fear to dictate your life?

"Say to those with fearful hearts, "be strong, and do not fear, for your God is coming to destroy your enemies. He is coming to save you"" Isaiah 35:4

Depression creates fear and can paralyzes the mind, preventing you from taking positive steps towards healing. Fear of the unknown and most importantly fear of not living up to your expectations can be depressing. Fear is the catalyst that holds a lot of people captive and in pain and in places where we remain mediocre failing to pursue God's purpose for our lives. Fear of the unknown keeps many millennial women from discovering their true calling. Maybe because you feel unworthy or are afraid of not living up to Gods entrusted purpose? On the other hand, it could be lack of faith. It may even be the fear of people. Pray to overcome fear during depression. Let God worry about the unknown, life is uncertain but with understanding of the word, you can embrace the uncertainties of life.

A life changing moment for me was when I decided to journey down the path God has assigned for me. I was still unsure and filled many questions and a lot of uncertainty. So I asked God "How do I do it? Who's going to help me get there?" Continuing on that path and living a life of obedience is a completely different ballgame. It takes consistent prayer, strength, focus, determination, persistence, and boldness. As the book of Hebrews encourages us,

"Let us hold tightly without wavering to the hope we affirm, for God can be trusted to keep his promise" (Hebrews 10:23)

Standing in faith when you face fear. Instead of giving in to fear of failure, hold on to faith. When all else fails let you faith reign over fear. *"I prayed to the Lord, and he answered me. He freed me from all my fears. Those who look to him for help will be radiant with joy; no shadow of shame will darken their faces. In my desperation I prayed and the Lord listened; he saved me from all my troubles."* Psalms 34:2-6

Failure can make or break you

How do you define failure?

The way you interpret your failure will either hinder or progress your life. Failure, rejection and setbacks are a part of life. Millennial woman, you cannot let life's circumstances bring you down, your reaction to circumstances can determine the course of your life. The way you process the failure is crucial to your success. With this. If you allow failure to define you, people feel that energy. And the more you dwell in that failure or setback, the more likely you are to remain in depression as life drives past you. If you focus on your past mistakes, it will leave you consumed with negative thoughts and regret. You might feel powerless to make the necessary changes, but the reality is that when you allow yourself to wallow in depression; you shut off the doors and prevent others from reaching in to help. Don't block off your healing. Praying to the Lord and be liberated by Him. Do not isolate yourselves when depression hits. That's exactly what the enemy wants. When we retreat into that black inner world, assuming no one understands we end up in the enemies trap: isolation, fixation on the past, refusal to get help, refusal to move forward in life.

Surrender and submit your burdens to God

Psalms 46:1-2 assures us, *"God is our refuge and strength, always ready to help in times of trouble. So we will not fear when earthquakes come and the mountains crumble into the sea."*

With professional counseling and a strong support group, I gradually regained strength to overcome my depression. I made up my mind—I would not be defined by having a husband and children, or by owning material things. I began to trust God like never before and that turning point revitalized my being. The miracles around me were evident God is omnipotent. As I surrendered control to God, the pressure to attain these goals came off my shoulders and I began to truly live in the present—to discover my purpose and live the life God intends for me. Finally, I could actively live a life full of purpose as I follow God's lead, rather than waiting for a man to rescue me. With my identity firmly rooted in God, I become unshakable. This is exactly how God wants us to live our lives, as the following verses remind us.

"Consider it pure joy, my brothers and sisters, whenever you face trials of many kinds, because you know that the testing of your faith produces perseverance. "Let's perseverance finish its work so that you may be mature and complete, not lacking anything." James 1:2-4

"Let your roots grow down into him, and let your lives be built on him. Then your faith will grow strong in the truth you were taught, and you will overflow with thankfulness." Colossians 2:7

In the ugly face of depression, you maybe tempted many times to give up on God, give up on life. All you can see before you is darkness and hopelessness. But trust God to lift you out of that pit. As you persevere through the suffering, you will become "mature and complete, not lacking anything." When you come out on the other side, you will be stronger and more ready to accomplish your calling.

So millennial woman, if you are struggling with depression, involuntarily living by the flesh or your own understanding. Ask for help in renewing your mind and a life of peace with God. The struggles we face are battles between the flesh and the spirit. The flesh thrives on instant gratification from worldly pursuits, but the spirit is eternal peace. The moment you let the flesh win, the devil takes over, but the spirit will never deceive you. It guides you to freedom.

Galatians 5:17 sums it up, *"For the flesh desires what is contrary to the Spirit, and the Spirit what is contrary to the flesh. They are in conflict with each other, so that you are not to do whatever you want."*

The importance of a strong support system

How strong is your core support system?

An important part of combating depression is having the right people around you at all times. When you are buried deep under depression, it is hard to comprehend the severity of the situation. Having a strong support system around will strengthen you suffocating in depression alone. Just like it takes a village to raise a child, it takes a village of supportive people who will pray and intercede for you to overcome situations in life. These people should be wise, so they know how best to pray for you and give you practical assistance. They come with firm roots in Christ, so they will pull from God's wisdom to help you. Depression is not a battle you can win on your own. Even if those people are not equipped to help, they'll be able to seek out resources to assist you. A support system is so important in life. Find people who have strong resources, wise, and strong in faith. Be very selective in choosing those in your support system. They have to be intercessors when you are weak and cheerleaders when you're winning with no jealousy.

Trust and obey for there is no other way

How deep is your trust in God?

"If we were tempted by such trials, we must not say, This temptation comes from God. "For God cannot be tempted by evil, and he himself tempts no one. But we are tempted when we are drawn away and trapped by our own evil desires."

So often, the problems we face are a result of our own stubbornness and failure to trust and obey God. Even after overcoming depression, I needed the spirit of wisdom and obedience more than ever due to temptations.

Surely, it takes dedication and a lot of strength to continue trusting and obeying God. But the effort is worth it! With God on your side, you don't need anyone's permission or validation. All the weight of the past—mistakes, failures—are shed at the foot of the cross. As you go forward, the road will be difficult, but there will no longer be burdens on your shoulder.

Dear millennial woman, I know the fight against depression is a long battle, but not impossible. With God all things are possible, trust in His goodness, reach out to those He's put in your life and ask them to lift you up in prayer. As God renews your mind, you will gain the strength to ignore the enemy's lies and march boldly through the cloud of depression. This process starts with you acknowledging your need for help and a support group. In the middle of the process, face the baggage of pressure points head on, and seek to understand where they came from. Then healing can begin, as you grow in strength and increase in your obedience and faith.

Be comforted that wherever the enemy is, God is present. I could have fallen many times into the devil's trap, but I fought on with God's hand over my life. His torch led me from darkness to light into His glory for my life. In your darkness, God is also there, ready to lead you out of it with His radiance.

"King David said this about him: 'I see that the LORD is always with me. I will not be shaken, for he is right beside me. No wonder my heart is glad, and my tongue shouts his praises! My body rests in hope.'" Acts 2:25-26

As children of God, we've received from him a spirit of stability and steadfastness that allow us to be unshaken in the face of Satan's taunting. With the help of the omnipresent God, the Spirit that dwells in us to conquer whatever comes our way. The devil will constantly try to deter you until your last breath. In both your misery and victory, the devil will be there. There were days when I just wanted to be alone, in those moments, I got creative in my journal and wrote out my thoughts and concerns to God. I chose to sulk in my misery a bit, which was the devil's work. However, after a few minutes, I quickly whispered, "God, help me." Shortly I would open the Bible and search the words *strength*, *encouragement*, *love*, and *perseverance*. Doing this would kept my spirit up and in some strange way, the days started getting better. God always showed up to pull me back. These are some of ways to bypass the negative thoughts on lonely days, search for scriptures and hold God accountable for those promises.

Confronting depression means digging up the unresolved issues you buried years ago. It can get messy and painful. But this is a necessary process to understand why certain things happened, what God's will for you is, and how you can learn from them and move on in your life. In this process you will learn to discern what is God's voice and what is the devil's voice. You will learn to listen to God and follow His guidance. That is the beginning of living the abundant life God has promised for us. The beginning of experiencing the power of God.

How social media contribute to the millennial woman's struggle

Everyone has a coping mechanism for dealing with the struggles of their day-to-day life, but there are times when our coping mechanism breaks down from the weight of one setback on top of another. If it has happened to you, it doesn't mean you are weaker or less capable than other people. We all have different trials in life, and some people simply have been given more difficult hills to climb. It is important to know the signs when your coping mechanism may not be sufficient, and get help if necessary. Although many people suffer from depression, some are all too often pressured by social media to keep up with others, to pretend we are okay when we are not, and to suffer in silence and solitude. But you do not have to live like that! God's plan for us is to thrive, in community with fellow Christians, and in honesty with ourselves and with other people.

Although God's intention is for Christians to love and support each other, unfortunately it is not always easy to talk about depression and suicide in the church. People might think you lack faith. They might just tell you to pray harder. They might judge you and think you're simply being punished for your disobedience. That is why we need more awareness about the truth of depression even in the church, so that people are empowered with the right tools to help their brothers and sisters. But there is hope, my dear sister. If you do not feel safe opening up to just anyone, you can seek spiritual counseling from a church leader. That's what I did. Spiritual counseling gave me the understanding and tools I needed to fight depression.

However, there may be times when you may need more than spiritual counseling. Some people suffer from a form of depression related to chemical imbalance in the brain, which requires medical intervention and treatment. However, this type of treatment is not always encouraged in some communities because of a lack of understanding and information. It is crucial for churches to educate their members about the truth of depression—that people who suffer from it are not weaker or lack faith. They may be under particularly intense attack by the enemy. To better minister to the growing population of people suffering from depression, churches should have a ministry specifically dedicated to spiritual counseling for depression, and get professional advice by partnering with the National Alliance on Mental Illness (NAMI) or any organization focused on mental health education.

Without a robust understanding of depression, family and friends might tell you to just "snap out of it." If only it were that easy! People need to understand that there are profound differences between normal sadness and depression. Until they understand that difference, you can't effectively cure the symptoms. While normal blues dissipate within a short amount of time, depression can lingers for months or even years resulting in substantial changes both physically and mentally: significant weight loss or weight gain within a short period, changes in eating habits, social isolation, suicidal thoughts, changes in sleep patterns, and feelings of hopelessness. When we are educated about depression, we can recognize these signs and help rescue our loved ones from sinking deeper. But so many people are not familiar with the symptoms of t depression, and by the time they realize, it may be too late to intervene.

What delivered me from depression was prayer and spiritual counseling. But there is a wide range of treatments to choose from, and everyone responds to these treatments differently. Some people find group counseling beneficial, while others benefit from individual counseling. Others recover within a short period after medical intervention, while others need to take psychotropic medicine for a longer time to manage their symptoms. But it is also clear that very often, especially in clinically depressed people, a combination of both medication and counseling maybe the most effective form of treatment. In the following pages I will present a brief description of different types of depression and the treatment options available to you, but there is much more information on community resource websites for you to look into.

Before diving into the various types of depression, I just want to mention again that my goal of sharing my testimony and what have learned along the way is to help others with similar experiences. My intent is to share the resources to aid in whatever form of depression you are enduring for those who are not suffering from depression but have loved ones who are, these resources can equip you to recognize the signs of depression and minister to those in need.

Types of Depression

Do you know anyone with symptoms of depression?

According to the NIH, major depression is the leading cause of disability in the U.S. and worldwide. Every year, depressive disorders affect an estimated 6.7% percent of adult Americans aged 18 and above, or about 15.7 million people in 2014—in the U.S. alone!

There are several types of depression: biological, cognitive, gender-based, co-occurrence, genetic (or epigenetic), and situational. Although the root causes of these types of depression are different, they all manifest in similar symptoms: persistent sadness, isolation, lack of interest and participation in activities you once enjoyed, feelings of emptiness and unworthiness, restlessness, irritability, constant anxiety, guilt, excessive sleep, lack of energy, hopelessness, delusions, repeated suicidal thoughts, body pains, and difficulty with concentration.

Biological depression occurs when a chemical imbalance, from either deficiency or overabundance of brain chemicals, prevents the neurotransmitters from functioning properly. **Cognitive depression** is a form of clinical depression that results from low self-esteem and negative thoughts—in other words, how people cognitively view themselves. Depression can also be **gender-specific.** According to the National Institutes of Health (NIH), women are statistically more likely to suffer from depression than men because of causes such as hormonal changes and stress from childbirth and menopause. **Co-occurring** depression is a type of depression accompanied by another medical condition, such as heart disease, cancer, diabetes, Parkinson's, Alzheimer's, or hormonal disorders. Family history of clinical depression can cause **genetic depression,** and other circumstances—such as financial problems, losing a loved one, or difficult live events—give rise to **situational depression.**

In addition to classifying depression according to its cause, we can also distinguish between different types of depression according to their severity, duration, or symptoms. According to the National Institute of Mental Health, under the National Institutes of Health, **major depression** is diagnosed when the symptoms are highly severe and hinder the individual's ability to work, sleep, enjoy life, or function as a normal person. It can be just one occurrence or several episodes during a person's lifetime. To meet the diagnosis of major depression, a person has at least five or more of the symptoms for at least two weeks. At a minimum, major depression usually lasts for at least six months if you do not seek counseling or treatment.

Minor depression, on the other hand, is when a patient has less than four of the symptoms and lasts for a minimum of two weeks. Atypical depression presents in symptoms of overeating or oversleeping, which lead to feelings of rejection or sadness. Dysthymia is a milder form of depression, with at least two symptoms of depression, which can last for years if not treated.

Psychotic depression is present when an individual is in a psychotic state showing symptoms of hallucinations and delusions. Postpartum depression (10% to 15% of all cases of depression) is only found in women, and presents after giving birth, when the woman becomes overwhelmed with the daily responsibilities and hormonal and physical changes. Seasonal affective disorder (SAD) is a form of depression that is developed during winter but the patient usually recovers when spring arrives. Bipolar disorder patients show symptoms of extreme low moods (depression) and other times extreme high moods ("mania").

It should be clear by now that what differentiates the normal blues from depression is that the "blues," or general sadness, only lasts for a short period of time and is usually due to a normal incident such as a bad day or a fight with a loved one. People can recover from the blues quickly and get resolution from the originating issue. But if a quick resolution is not achieved, such as a prolonged reaction to a trauma or a loss, a person may gradually slide into depression.

Depression affects every aspect of your life and your loved ones. By pretending to be happy, the depression will only worsen and you will only become more isolated. The depression will drain your energy (changes in eating and sleeping habits), warp your perspective of life and yourself (ruminations of the past and anxiety about the future), and close off your outlook on life (suicidal ideations). Praying allows God to intervene, and with every ounce of energy, try to open up to someone. Sometimes, praying it away on your own does not work because the disease plagues the mind causing you to withdraw from loved ones. It is critical for our communities to be educated in this matter so when they notice behavioral changes, they can help get the right help. From my personal experience and talking to others who have suffered from depression, it is not easy to self-diagnose, but there are certain patterns in people who have prolonged depression.

If you think you may have depression, it is important that you reach out to a mental health professional, a spiritual leader, or a trusted friend. The conversations will not be easy, but unfortunately, depression will not go away on its own. Just know that no problem is too small or big for God to fix if you open up to Him for help. If you are not sure where to begin, simply pick up the Bible and see how the Spirit will illuminate your path, or contact the organizations listed at the end of this book. If you think you might need urgent help, call 1-800-273-TALK (8255) or go to www.suicidepreventionlifeline.org.

Healing from depression

If you are not suffering from depression, but know someone who is, please reach out and contact these organizations on your friend's behalf. People who suffer from depression often do not have the strength to reach out for help on their own. Healing and complete recovery is possible. Do not let depression consume you. With the right help, you can emerge and continue to pursue God's purpose in your life. When you emerge, your healing is a story that bears testament to God's great work.

When you reach out and begin to heal from depression, you will need to be honest and less critical of yourself. We are our own worst critics. Allow yourself time to overcome the challenges as you seek help. Do not rush the process; doing so can sabotage your progress. The beginning is a fragile process but with short-term goal assessments, you can overcome this disease. Learn to forgive yourself if you backslide and follow through according to plan. Give yourself room to grow and heal from setbacks constructively and healthily.

Allow yourself to grow with patience in the counseling process. Don't expect to be cured overnight— be it counseling or medication, all takes time to work. While some Christians oppose the use of antidepressants, I believe it is a legitimate treatment option, because God has given us the intellect and ability to create medical treatment. In addition, You cannot diagnose yourself. Medical professionals provide very effective treatment

that is their gift and God has put them in our society for
the very purpose of healing us.

It is important to be patient with the healing process,
it's good to set reasonable, short-term expectations for
yourself and take baby steps to build up on those goals.
Be ready to be flexible to lifestyle changes to progress
your healing. The healing process will challenge you to
grow in unexpected ways. Avail yourself of the counsel of
God, the expertise of the mental health professionals, and
the love and care of your support group. It can also be
healthy and conducive to recovery when you keep busy
in a healthy way by spending time with friends and
family or even taking on new hobbies. These positive
activities will keep your mind away from negative
thoughts.

Depression is treatable. So if you are suffering, or
know anyone who is, please seek help before it's too late.
Many professionals are ready to help. Below, please find a
list of resources you can turn to for help with
understanding and coping with depression.

Organizations to Help with Depression and Other Mental Illness:
National Alliance on Mental Health (NAMI)
Internet Address: http://www.NAMI.org

National Institute of Mental Health (NIMH)
Phone Number(s): (301) 496-9576
Internet Address: http://www.nimh.nih.gov

Depression After Delivery, Inc.
Phone Number(s): (800) 944-4773
Internet Address:
http://www.depressionafterdelivery.com

American Psychological Association (APA)
Phone Number(s): (800) 374-2721
Internet Address: http://www.apa.org

CHAPTER 6:
Breaking up with the old self

There were times in my life when my foundation was wavering, giving fertile soil for the enemy to take roots. I allowed people and noises of the society to influence my decision making, which led me down a path of insecurity and lack of self-esteem. I sought validation from people and was always disappointed. Living my life according to my plans was not working out well at all.

But when I thought all was lost, the Lord blessed me with something priceless: my purpose. I had always wanted to find out, "Why am I here?" but I never did the work to discover what I was meant to do. But I realized that God will never let me down as long as my purpose is aligned with His—if I am pursuing His will, I cannot be let down because God will always accomplish His will! I made a choice to pray for healing and mind renewal. I made the decision to stay alive. Sometimes it takes hitting rock bottom for people to finally realize that God had been trying to get their attention. It certainly took that much for me to come to that realization, the realization that the life I wanted only God could provide.

Distractions and judgements during your metamorphosis

Are you holding on to old habits that are hindering your growth?

During the process of returning to God, people may enter into our life during our metamorphosis either because they are sent to help propel us out of our suffering, or because they are sent by the to distract us. How do you know who is who? If they do not try to understand what you are going through and judge you according to your season of suffering or transformation, they are definitely there to distract you. Align with the right people who encourage and counsel you in those times of your transformation. They will help keep you accountable and push you through the process. At times, you may feel stuck in some stages of your metamorphosis due to distractions of depression, hopelessness or lack of dependence on God. Continue to pray for discernment to help you distinguish between those who are for you and against. Cease to allow their judgment of your current situation impact your progress or healing. Their criticism will only keep you in a vicious cycle of doubt, suffering, and depression.

God wants to relieve you of all your worries so you can live a life full of grace and favor. There is no other way to a content and fruitful life than through the creator. Look around you—the stars, planets, everything around you has been intricately created for a purpose.

You, too, were made specifically for a purpose and for His glory, and God will not abandon you. He is all you need to survive. What you think is impossible, God will make possible.

Consistency in prayer is key to finding peace and understanding during the healing process, God will reveal your strengths and gifts in order to maximize your potential. Those emotional issues holding you back from God's assignment will become a stepping-stone for your purpose. Understanding and accepting your strengths and weaknesses are key to finding purpose. In moments of weakness, be steadfast, pray for help, and allow God to direct your steps. It may even take asking God to connect you to the right messengers for help. Be vulnerable and humble enough to allow people in to see you at your weakest. Sometimes it is in your weakness that God reveals your purpose. As a millennial woman, you cannot allow your setbacks to overshadow your strengths, doing so creates distrust in the Holy Spirit to guidance. Distrust in God causes the enemy to sneak in doubt leading to lack of confidence in God and prompting you to make preliminary life changing decisions out of fear. As a result, you delay yourself from finding your purpose.

Healing is a choice

Are you ready to heal God's way?

"A glad heart makes a happy face; a broken heart crushes the spirit." Proverbs 15:13

Dear Millennial woman, know that healing is a choice and as you surrender to God, you will realize the choices you make determine your destiny. You can either allow the pain to take control of your life or accept God's will. There's a tendency to let the pain of failure, rejection and heartbreak take over but eventually you will have to face the emotional repercussions in order to grow spiritually. The best solution is to surrender and say "YES God, I want to do things your way".

By fighting against the light and truth of God, we try to take control of our own lives and when things fall apart, blame God. The constant shift of blame also delays our blessings and progress because the lesson we failed to learn from the failure is now recycled and will have to be re-lived in a new situation. Failure, rejection and heartbreak leaves one with a pool of questions like: why did my partner break up with me? Why am I not good enough? What did I do wrong? With each question you may overthink and feel powerless as one heartbreak follows another. Sometimes God has to expose the cracks in every area your life to get our attention and to focus on Him.

Comparison is the thief of joy

Part of the reason we struggle sometimes is depending on a man's love rather than depending on God. All of us have at one point or another failed to depend on God for our identity. Sometimes we forget the immense love of our Creator has for us as we pursue the temporary love of man. It is vital to remember you are love. You were

wonderfully made, as stated in Psalms 139:14, and no one
can take that from you unless you allow them. We do not
need to strive to be someone else to earn God's love. Jesus
made sure of that when he died for our sins. Let your self-
perception reflect God's infinite love.

At some point in the millennial woman's life, there is
the tendency to compare yourself to others or allow
negative experiences to define you, instead of rooting our
identity securely in God. You may even become anxious
and in a hurry to find a husband, start a family or find the
dream job. After all, these are promises of God right? I
know it becomes harder to digest as your friends enter
into that phase of life where they are getting married and
having children. It may seem like God is delaying your
blessings and you always come in last place. But rest
assured the waiting period is to test and prepare you for
your purpose. It can get discouraging at times, trust me I
know but know that God has your back. He is generous,
and will increase your territory of blessings, so surrender
and give up your fears.

Dear millennial woman, I pray you don't retreat into
a bubble of negative thoughts by allowing comparison
and obsessions de-powered you or sucked up all your
energy, turning even the simplest activities into
excruciating tasks. Don't allow the enemy to takeover
your mind, with landmines of negative thoughts
exploding by the minute. Put on that breastplate armor
of God and defeat the enemy!

Depression does not discriminate

What are some of your trigger points that cause you to doubt God's timing?

"We can rejoice, too, when we run into problems and trials, for we know that they help us develop endurance. And endurance develops strength of character, and character strengthens our confident hope of salvation. And this hope will not lead to disappointment. For we know how dearly God loves us, because he has given us the Holy Spirit to fill our hearts with his love." Romans 5:3-5

You might think that you're very strong and depression could never touch you. The reality, however, is that depression does not discriminate between gender, age, race, class, education level, wealth, or even internal strength. Depression can hit anyone. Elijah, the prophet of great faith, also struggled with a period of depression after winning a showdown against the prophets of Baal, which culminated with Elijah calling down fire from the heavens to consume the false prophets. Even after such a miraculous act, he fell into such a deep depression that he asked God to end his life. If it happened to a prophet, then everyone should be vigilant and on guard against depression.

Take a look at the passage about Elijah's struggle with depression, try to understand how a prophet of such anointing could become so distressed after a victory. The only answer I came up with is that he probably forgot his identity, mission, and how important his assignment was in his time. Similarly at times, we tend to forget the Lord's blessings around us, and instead focus on what we lack. That is why it is essential to stay in the word and in

Gods presence at all times. When we allow our mind to believe lies, that's when we begin to lose sight of God's goodness and slide into depression. Fight to look around you for the blessings you have now and thank Him for allowing you to see another day.

Cease to rush ahead of God

Do you need to breaking away from yourself?

"All praise to God, the Father of our Lord Jesus Christ. God is our merciful Father and the source of all comfort. He comforts us in all our troubles so that we can comfort others. When they are troubled, we will be able to give them the same comfort God has given us. For the more we suffer for Christ, the more God will shower us with his comfort through Christ. Even when we are weighed down with troubles, it is for your comfort and salvation! For when we ourselves are comforted, we will certainly comfort you. Then you can patiently endure the same things we suffer. We are confident that as you share in our sufferings, you will also share in the comfort God gives us." 2 Corinthians 1:3-7

I hope this passage reminds you who to look to everyday, especially in times of trials. I hope that it reminds you that even in the face of adversity, there are lessons to gain. I realized I rushed my past relationship into something that takes time and commitment. Rushing into marriage is a sure way to end in divorce and regret. Although the breakup was painful, I realized I dodged a bullet. It made me question, "What else had I been rushing all these years?" What else did I needed to change? I began asking myself a series of questions to dig deep into my core to find out what needed re-assessed.

I decided to break up with my old self when I realized my heart was not in the on God. My mind was always on Him but my heart was miles away. What was my old self like? I was the millennial woman who obsessed over having everything. In my twenties, I thought I had life perfectly planned, with an identity formed on happiness from marriage, house full children and a good 9 to 5. The old self insisted on leaning on my own understanding. It was ruled by fear and disappointments similar to what some millennial women face. Those plans never came into fruition because I was rushing and manipulating plans to fit into God's plans. I learned the hard way God does not need our approval.

When our plans backfire, we tend to shut people out of our world because we're afraid they'll judge or abandon us If they see your mistakes. Dear Millennial woman, there's no need to hide, mistakes are made for you to learn and give up your stubborn ways to God. If you wait on God, He will go over and beyond the expectation of your desires. I urge you millennial women to bring your failures to God. Do not undervalue your worth. When you are truly dependent on God, He will graciously open your eyes to see yourself as a reflection of love. This will help you bury the old way of thinking as you begin to seek out your identity in Christ, with a renewed mindset

"No, dear brothers and sisters, I have not achieved it, but I focus on this one thing: Forgetting the past and looking forward to what lies ahead. I press on to reach the end of the race and receive the heavenly prize for which God, through Christ is calling us." Philippians 3:13-14

I hope this passage resonates with you as you release your old self and you are renewed as a strong self-assured millennial woman. The restoration will give you the confidence only grace can provide. Know that no matter the magnitude of your struggles, you can always bring them to God in prayer, and petition. He will restore you. The time to unleash your burdens is now. Stop finding excuses like "this isn't the right time." There is no better time to let God take control of your life than now.

The cost of not letting go of your old self is incalculable. If you continue to live with fear, failure, rejection and heartbreak, you hold yourself hostage. Dear millennial woman, stop inflicting unnecessary pain to yourself and give it to God.

When people refuse to break up with their old self, it can be ego (thinking they have it all under control) or low self-esteem (undervaluing their worth). Both kinds of people need God. The prideful should realize that whatever they can gain with their own strength could not even remotely compare to what God has in store. The timid should trust that God has already equipped you with power to operate in confidence and boldness. Do not let your pride or fear stop you from fulfilling your purpose.

As I have tried to explain thus far in this book, there is freedom and complete liberty when you give up control. When you let go of your old self, God renews you from within and prepares you to live your destined life. That is when your life's purpose becomes a reality. As you allow God to gradually build up your new identity, you begin to attract positive energy. It is a completely different existence from living by your own might. The negativity, fear, impulse to compare are all a waste of time. They slowed down your blessings. They paralyze all efforts of growth. When you bury the old self, there's a lightness in your step. There dwells hope, faith, and joy.

The mind is the most powerful tool in the body.

Your thoughts can control you. They can either destroy you or build you up. But there is no possible way to exercise your mind in a positive way, if you are enslaved to the old habits of disobedience. When you let it all go, and allow God to take over, you will see how high and wide He can take you. The ride with the Lord is never ending. All He asks for is trust and faith.

Breaking up with your old self means being reborn and leaving negative perceptions of your past where they belong. Just like combatting depression, you will need a strong support group to help you stay committed. Without strong and wise people to hold you accountable, it can be tempting to return to your old self. You must resist the temptation to retreat to those old ways. As the Spirit breathes new life into you, you will renew in the mind and spirit. Dear millennial woman, be encouraged to endure trials and tribulations and emerge victorious.

Be still and allow God to preparing your heart to feed your faith. Know that He is always one step ahead, paving the way for you to reach your harvest and victory. God does not punish rather he corrects and straightens your path. He will strengthen you spiritually, mentally, and physically. Dear millennial woman, trust that I know the healing can be painful but the reward from God far exceeds the storm. Every struggle during the process provides lessons that strengthen your faith. Healing God's way is never vain, it is the beginning for a greater gift.

CHAPTER 7:

Renewing the mind and healing god's way

Break me, Heal Me, Mold me, Use Me
It is time to stop looking at your brokenness as a weakness. With prayer you can set the stage for God to heal, mold and use you for a purpose. Your brokenness can be the key to finding your purpose. Don't settle for a temporary fix, put the little ounce of faith you got left into action and pray on it. Ask God to take every broken piece of your heart, heal it, and fill it with His unconditional love. Millennial woman, you no longer need the love of people according to the flesh, instead run after the ever the omnipresent love of God.

Exactly what happens in the middle of that process will vary from person to person, depending on their unique struggles. But I venture to say that for everyone, it will take tremendous sacrifice and determination, and the willingness to be vulnerable and allow God to penetrate

our heart to do His work. For everyone, the process will
look similar to this:

1. God will first break us by allowing us to
   undergo trials;
2. He will then heal us as we hand over control to
   Him;
3. He will mold us into His likeness as we learn to
   boldly stand up again and live out His purpose
   for us; and finally,
4. He will enable us to love again by using our
   testimonies to bless many people.

Every step of this process requires walking with the
Spirit. You cannot progress from one stage to the next if
you live in the flesh. The process won't be easy but the
Spirit will guide you at all the times. Some days are
harder than others with thoughts of uncertainty but with
the Spirit guiding you, push through the process, your
breakthrough is around the corner.

Temptations in the process of stillness

I met a man who wanted and was willing to give me
everything I once craved for: marriage, kids, and a white
picket-fenced house but the timing was all wrong and
because I no longer defined my existence with those
things, I saw the red flags. Discernment kicks in when
things are too good to be true. Seeking God's approval
becomes second nature and you'll want to pursue God's
purpose first. Millennial woman, if I don't fully heal
you'll end up jumping into relationships without the
right tools and the void will remain. Making the decision

not to be with him at that moment took tremendous strength and wisdom but I knew I was definitely getting stronger and felt God's guiding hand. I could not pursue a relationship with this man because he wanted me skip some crucial steps. You simply cannot rush God. Trusted the spirit to guide you in making the right decisions.

Brokenness is a silent gift

"Keep on asking, and you will receive what you ask for. Keep on seeking, and you will find. Keep on knocking, and the door will be opened to you. For everyone who asks, receives. Everyone who seek, finds. And to everyone who knocks, the door will be opened." Matthew 7:7

As you move from brokenness to recovery, there will be things to deter you and people who are impatient and want to rush the process for you. Do not allow them to get in the way. Be patient with yourself and be patient with God. Your perseverance will be all worth it.

"Do not copy the behavior and customs of this world, but let God transform you into a new person by changing the way you think. Then you will learn to know God's will for you, which is good and pleasing and perfect." Romans 12:2

As you begin the process of healing, the first thing you will encounter is utter brokenness. Sometimes that is what God has to do to humble us and help us see that we need Him. When God saved me from myself and preserved my life, He spoke to me and assured me that He has a purpose for me, but that He had to break me first so I could be humbled enough to trust Him. One night, I remember reading the story of King David when he lost everything, including his wives, children, and possessions, to the Amalekites. After crying and mourning, David found strength in the Lord and God restored him.

Let that story uplift your spirit—if God restored King David, then surely He will restore you too. Whatever situation you're facing has a purpose and in due time start making sense. Be eager to endure the process in order to find your purpose. By remaining still, God reveal some things to you.

In that stillness is where your story of redemption will begin, your character, resilience, and patience will increase for your next level. And most importantly, the revelation of God's purpose for your life. With an awakened purpose in life, You'll begin to carve out a new existence.

Millennial woman, you are a work in progress, pray for God to mold you in his vision and let your testimony prove the true in the following passages, be the change others need.

A renewed mind penetrates the soul

"Let your roots grow down into him, and let your lives be built on him. Then your faith will grow strong in the truth you were taught, and you will overflow with thankfulness." Colossians 2:7

As you go through the process of the renewal of your mind, and heal in God's way, be assured that God has given you not a spirit of boldness. You can boldly approach the throne of grace to ask for strength to fight off old tendencies and the attacks of the enemy. A renewed mind encompasses a new spirit of authority, steadfastness and fearlessness. You begin to live outside your comfort zone as you prepare to embrace God's purpose. In time, God will reveal a plan completely different from what you have envisioned for yourself. But you have to trust that God knows better than you do, and He is taking you in a new direction, more beautiful than the path you carved out for yourself. After all, He created you with specific gifts for an assignment only you can fulfill. That is why you are one of a kind. So trust God, embrace it as He molds you into the instrument appropriate for His purposes. It may be painful to let go of your plans and accept that you are actually meant to do something completely different, but healing is metamorphosis—though painful, you will emerge more powerful and radiant than before. Take comfort in the psalmist's words:

"He heals the broken hearted and bandages their wounds" (Psalm 147:3)

God uses different ways to renew our minds. For some people, their minds are renewed by talking it out with friends, family, or a therapist. For others, the process takes place primarily in solitude or a combination of both. For me, it was in the solitude of reading the Bible day and night that my mind was transformed. There will be nights of crying out to God and you will be lead directly to a particular passage. You will be lead to read devotional materials addressing your circumstance, reminding you to let go and trusting in God's faithfulness.

Regardless of how God renews your mind and heals your heart, you will likely go through three stages, beginning with anger and self-accusation. When you find yourself deep in distress and trouble, your instinct is to find out who is to blame: yourself, or someone else? Whoever it is, someone caused this debacle. But at this stage, you are not focusing on your issues or needs. You are not focusing on how to heal and move forward. God will gently bring you out of this stage into the second stage: acknowledgment and healing. He will help you focus on the areas in your life that are broken, all your past issues and setbacks, everything that needs to be healed and restored. Finally, you will enter into the stage of awakening—awakening to the fact that God put you through your storms for the reason of breaking you down in order to build, mold you and use you.

Obviously, the middle stage tends to be the messiest time of the healing process. It is when God reveals all kinds of ugly issues buried deep in your soul, and compels you to come face to face with them. You will need to pray for strength. Ask God to persevere and deal with the issues that must be resolved in order for you to be renewed. Remember that God restored countless people in the Bible and used them to accomplish great things: David, Jonah, Joseph, Elizabeth, Sarah, Hannah, Mary, among many others. Of course, you also need to ask for strength and wisdom to guard against Satan, who will be there to deceive you.

1 Peter 5:7 says, "Give all your worries and cares to God, for he cares about you."

When the Lord pointed me to this verse, I knew it was not by chance. The Holy Spirit wanted to remind me that God was present and in charge. Every step of the way as I was being renewed, every time I felt tempted to return to my old self, God was right there to sustain me. I am certain that He will do the same for you, because He is a promise-keeping, gracious, and generous God.

It is important that you turn to God in prayer not just when you are in trouble. As we heal, we must stay in constant communication with God, praying and asking the Holy Spirit to show us where we needed to grow, what we needed to do differently. To hear God's response to your questions, it takes more than just talking to Him. You must eliminate the noise in life to be able to hear Him clearly. From the start of my healing process, cut off as much noise and distraction as you can from TV, social media, radio, and those disturbing your peace in order to hear God clearly.

What noises or distractions do you need to cut out from your life in order to hear God's voice more clearly?

Being healed and renewed is a wonderful thing, because the very purpose of healing and renewal is to make us stronger people. God does not heal us to remain in the same place but to testify of his goodness and bless others. He heals us so that we are more mature and better equipped to help others who are going through the trials. The more you help others, the more you become healed, because you shift the focus from yourself , and as you minister to others after your renewal, you will be planting seeds of greatness in others, which will one day be harvested for many other people's joyfulness.

In fact, even before you are completely healed, God can begin to use you in great ways because you are already aligned with His purposes. I was amazed that God was using me to serve others even though I was not completely healed myself. I encountered many people who suffered from depression or setbacks and after spending time with them and explaining the tools I was given to heal, they were inspired to pray more and seek God's presence in their lives. Being spirit led to help others is fulfilling and now I stood strong, able to laugh and be present with others while helping them. I God uses us who are broken to accomplish great things! Just think how much more can we do for God when our healing and renewal is complete?

We may want to hide our pain and pretend to be strong. However, when we try to be genuine and vulnerable, when we are not afraid to share with others our struggles, it can be a powerful living testimony for others to see when God transforms us from our worst to a new self. When we allow other people into our lives, they will be able to see with their very eyes how God is working to change and heal us. However, not every redemption story is meant to be made public. Sometimes the circumstances may require that the story be tucked away from the public eye until things have calmed down. You must exercise your judgment and consult your spiritual leader or counselor to decide how much of your story to disclose to other people, if at all.

Healing God's way is the the way to ensure spiritual and mental stability. When God penetrates your mind, body and soul, your awareness is awakened therefore you are more conscious of how you use time, aligning with the right people and always allocate time in conversation with Him each day. In everything you do, you'll know if God is present or guiding you through. Healing is the power to trust, love and fearlessly pursue our dreams. A broken mind or heart unattended spiritually can destroy a person. The point is God wants to you to be restored, whole, and in authority for his army.

As you heal, trust that God can turn you into His instrument, no matter your past failures or disappointent. Don't worry about people judging you, where the carnal world sees failure God finds an opportunity to turn the situation into a song of victory. Saul (Paul) used to be a leader of persecution against Christians, but even he was changed into one of the most anointed servants of God. Surely you, too, can be transformed and healed from your past.

The process of healing and renewal differs in length per individual but staying committed is key, a break in service will delay your progress so it is vital to cut all distractions for the duration until your mind is completely renewed and the heart is full. There will be times of fear or doubt but trust me the Spirit is with you every step of the way. With a renewed mind there's an overflow in blessings, energy, power and most importantly the zeal to get closer to God and pursue your purpose.

CHAPTER 8:
There is purpose in every failure

Submit your heart and mind to God and free yourself

"Charm is deceptive, and beauty is fleeting; but a woman who fears the Lord is to be praised. Honor her for all that her hands have done, and let her works bring her praise at the city gate." Proverbs 31:30

Something about pain that drives one to seek a deeper understanding of life's purpose. In the reconstruction phase, you will begin to see life with a sharper lens, which will cause you to reflect back on other failed attempts to race ahead of God's plans. I recommend you take time to pray and seek God's will for your life. Seeking purpose in the midst of chaos and setbacks means facing fear in a gladiator's arena, and kicking it in the face. You have to fight to work with God as He heals and molds you into someone who truly fears Him. Someone who no longer runs after what the world says are good. Someone who only runs after the Lord and His will.

Millennial woman, know that God has already equipped you with a purpose, and it is up to each individual to seek and nurture it. You've been sitting on your purpose this whole time and maybe God had to put you through a test before finally getting the lessons to infuse that purpose. Seek within yourself, to want to live for God. Many of our problems are tests to awaken our purpose. If the lesson is learned then there will be purpose in the problem. Seek and find your calling, it is already within you. No one can fulfill that purpose, but you, because you are a chosen one. You were created with that purpose in God's image.

Finding and pursuing God's purpose can mean giving up everything you once thought was vital for my existence. Persevere the growing pains of the dry season and focus on self-development. Its also means saying no to mediocrity and slaying your fears to get to your ideal self filled with meaning and passion. Living a life according to God's purpose means total surrender and knowing you cannot serve God's purpose with a hidden agenda. Commit with your mind and heart. Sometimes we fail to connect the two and only flow with partial submission to God. God doesn't need help so stop trying to convince him to approve your plans. Self-made plans are acts of the flesh and focus on instant gratification. That kind of half-hearted obedience will lead you astray and have you serving time in the pit confusion. Millennial woman you are wiser than that, crawled out with blood, sweat, and tears. Don't trust yourself to make decisions or plan a life without God. There are many amongst us who do the same, faithfully attend church on Sundays, along with Bible Study and every class yet only committed on a part-time basis. Seeking help from God on a needed basis. Give up your double life and reach for the all knowing creator. God is ready and open to receive you, the whole being not just the mind, but your heart too.

When you come to terms with the dangers of partial submission, you have to ask for forgiveness and ask God to instill obedience and a committed spirit over your life. Sometimes it take falling flat to know you have to surrender. Seek your purpose and adhere to His vision for your life. With God there is no kicking and screaming, complaining about life not turning out the way you wanted it to because it becomes easier to comply. Millennial woman, I urge you to burn those plans and focus on, Proverbs 19:21 that tells us clearly, *"You can make many plans, but the Lord's purpose will prevail."*

Discovering your purpose

Exodus 9:16 *"But I have spared you for a purpose, to show you my power and to spread my fame throughout the earth."*

Discovering your purpose is a rebirth and implementing calls for training, building character and commitment. Dear Millennial women, don't rush to execute what God hasn't installed. Let God walk you through lesson needed with each step. At times you may feel overwhelmed not know how, when, where but you must stay focused and patient. The first step is praying for

the resources you need to invest in your purpose. This
will require so jotting down what it will take to achieve
those goals. It may take enrolling back in school and
taking courses to enhance your understanding of your
assignment. Taking those actions must become a habit
and a constant force to move you forward in order to
fulfill God's assignment. Having a clear vision and a solid
plan to achieve that vision gradually builds character
helps you become sensitive to God's voice.

Prayer after discovery and messengers

*"Hope deferred makes the heart sick but a dream fulfilled is a tree
of life."* Proverbs 13:12

Deep down, we all know there's a greater purpose, a
purpose God has designed for us, with our name on it.
Millennial woman, know that you are not here just to
exist or accumulate material things in pursuit of instant
gratification. You will experience profound joy and peace
that will permeated your soul after your rebirth. Focus all
your energy on achieving God's purpose. Since the hard
work comes after discovery, you need to be steadfast with
your prayer life. Is may require setting up a prayer closet
where you can spend intimate time with God.

Slay the noise

No matter how meticulously we plan our lives to
have things happen in specific timeframe, God
orchestrates our lives and only He knows how each day

will end. Our true purpose is to worship and praise God, and be content with whatever unique purpose God has for us individually. Surround yourself with people who will help you discover your calling, rather than letting too many people drown you with all kinds of voice and opinions. Do not allow distracting noises to offset your balance or confuse you in your quest. It is important to be cautious in spreading yourself too thin, focusing too much on helping those in profound needs before you are ready. There are those needy people in your life (the takers) who will deplete the energy you need for your growth. When you renew and focus, you will be better able to serve and minister to others effectively. It is vital to be selective in whom you surround with.

Another reason to be selective with whom you allow into your support group is that not everyone can join you on the path God is taking you. Your new path will require new networks of people working collectively for God's purpose. Due to the magnitude of responsibility and uniqueness of your path, you will have to disassociate yourself from some people. In your rebirth, you can never be common in your associations with certain people. God will guide you with discernment and will help you stay your course to move forward on your strictly aligned course. You will be able to decipher the good and toxic relationships. Those in good company will uplift you while others may jump on board with their own personal agendas. The journey is not easy, and we cannot afford to let naysayers deter us from pursuing God.

Be courageous in pursuing your purpose

In the beginning you may be overwhelmed with the responsibility assigned and when that happens, and you find yourself faltering in your pursuit of God's purpose, all you need to do is whisper, "Jesus, I need your help. Direct my steps." God always comes through to give us the strength we need to press on. Do not be overwhelmed by the distance you have to travel. Although it may seem like an impossible goal from where you are, believe that with God nothing is impossible and that life is a race to be completed with a series of baby steps. Do not ask "How do I get there?" Of course, we all ask that question but we just have to focus on putting one foot in front of the other, and trust God to bring about the healing and renewal in His prefect timing. The Lord says if you acknowledge Him in all your ways, He will direct your path. I firmly believe God will show us the way as we seek Him.

Pursuing and living God's purpose takes courage and determination. Be determined to live out your purpose after He reveals it to you. That purpose may be unfamiliar and it will require you to stretch your faith out of your comfort zone, but it will only be for growth and benefit. If you choose not to live out God's purpose, however, you will end up back in the awkward cycle. And by going against God's will, you may take yourself down the rabbit hole of disappointment & failures. Your blessing is in your purpose.

Initially, your purpose may seem much bigger than yourself, but rest assured God knows what He is doing and He will not throw confusion in the mix ever! You may not physically feel you are capable but God has already equipped you mentally and physically, your faith determines your success. He has chosen you for a reason. The spirit will guide you, as long as you stay in your destined lane. You only need to trust Him to guide you step by step. When you surrender yourself to God's will, God will use you for greater things than you can ever imagine. Whatever talents and abilities you have now, God will develop them to their fullest potential. Years from now, you will look back amazed at the course of your journey, your testimony will inspire others to seek life through Christ. It will be victorious and sweet journey as you continue to grow in faith. People will be able to recognize God's grace on your life's journey, and they will be infused with zeal to seek to God's will.

Spiritual Gifts

Do you know your spiritual gifts?

"For he will complete what he appoints for me, and many such things are in his mind." Job 23:14

God has given each of us a gift from his great variety of spiritual gifts. Do you have the gift of speaking? Then speak as though God himself were speaking through you with boldness and confidence. Do it with all the strength and energy that God supplies, do not neglect your gifts. Your purpose will reveal your gifts in due time. Spiritual gifts are to be used with extra care. Know when exercise them through guidance of the Holy Spirit. Then everything you do will bring glory to God through Jesus Christ" 1 Peter 4:10

As you begin to fulfill God's purpose, you must go forth with determination. Do not delay and find excuses for your hesitation. Sure, the journey ahead is full of unknowns. God wants you to do things you cannot imagine being able to do. He wants you to step outside of your comfort zone. He will not leave you by yourself to fight it all alone. When God is transitioning you into a new creation, He will send you helpers or people to speak on your behalf, just like Ruth and Naomi or Elijah and Elisha. God will set the stage for doors to be open for you in order to fulfill your purpose.

The first step in any change is always the hardest. Once you ask for God for strength and take that first step, it will become easier. You will learn and adjust to your gifts and doing things God's way. It will be as strange to embrace the unknown or to trust God in an unfamiliar situation. Grow to trust God and truly surrender your life to Him. In time, your gifts will show that Christ, not man, defines your identity. Your story will be a clear statement that your identity is unshakeable, firm, and glorious in Christ. No earthly setback can diminish your value.

Beware; the enemy knows your purpose too

As you learn to rely on God and allow His vision to manifest through your life, you will experience some of the greatest attacks. You see, the enemy knows your purpose too, and will do all he can to distract you. He will try to divert you with physical, mental, financial, or spiritual attacks. He may even tempt you into thinking you can fulfill God's purpose without God's help. He did this very thing with our Lord Himself. Mathew 4:1-11 talks about the devil tempting Jesus to bow down to him and tricking Jesus into believing He does not need God to have riches or power. Jesus resisted that temptation, and with God's help, you can, too. Remember that we are nothing apart from Christ. We must stay focused on God. The closer you are to God, obedience becomes second nature, therefore you become wiser, stronger and able to overcome the evil one.

What God intends for you may be in a totally foreign territory than what you had in mind. As God enlarges your territory, He will equip you with tools to overcome every situation. Your purpose may demand a set of new skills in order to develop some qualities to do Gods work. Do not get frustrated about living in this foreign territory, for as God led Abraham, he will guide and stretch you to master the tools needed to get your purpose accomplished. Resist the urge to jump the gun before you are ready. Be patient as God teaches you. Persevere through this process with patience, and it will develop your temperament and character into master. Jesus spoke on this very point:

"When the Spirit of truth comes, he will guide you in all truth. He will not speak on his own but will tell you what he has heard. He will tell you about the future. He will bring me glory by telling you whatever he receives from me. All that belongs to the Father is mine; this is why I said, 'The Spirit will tell you whatever he receives from me." John 16:13-15

Dear millennial woman, be patient, follow the guidance and counsel of the Holy Spirit, and trust that the God who started the good work in you will see you through to the finish line.

Slay doubt when walking in your purpose

Millennial woman, as you journey through life, there will be times where you may doubt your purpose as the fear of the unknown crowds your mind. During these times, you may ask "God, do you really believe in me that much to give this assignment?" This is normal as you build confidence in Him. You are not alone, we all go through this stage, in fact, your purpose should scare you. You may be filled with doubt and insecurities. When this happen kneel in prayer, and ask for clarity. He will increase your confidence and growing desire for peace. One terrifying thing about running towards your purpose is the fate of the unknown, the unknown turns into fear. Learn to slay your fears! Slaying fear and dominating doubt with faith is liberating and powerful.

I am nowhere near, where God wants to take me but every day I make progress with God's plan for that day inching toward the assignment God has set before me. As I grow to serve God, I reflect on how much time and effort I wasted in the past on accumulating materials things and finding validation in people. I am thankful and feel empowered, after trading my fears for a life full of blessings possibilities. Allow God to do the same for you.

The grunt work

Are you ready to work?

As millennial women, we all want a life worth living and hope to leave a mark on this earth but many of us are not willing to do the grunt work. Some people may struggle to surrender to God completely. They might think, "Sure, I'll follow God's way, but I'll put my spin on it." If you have any inclination like this, you must ask the Spirit to slay those temptations. That is a sign that you are still living in the flesh. God has given us intellect and wisdom, and the ability to make certain decisions in life. However, we cannot trust ourselves to be the architect of our lives. Doing so, is a predestined match with destruction. God requires total surrender because He is all knowing. He knows exactly what we need and the applicable time. When we try to intervene and force things to happen our way, we will only be meddling in God's work. Don't waste time trying to figure things out on your own seek counsel. The time to follow God *completely*—is now.

As we seek and fulfill God's purpose, we should inquire after God often, as King David did. He asked God whether he should chase down the Philistines after they raided his town and took everything, including his wives and children. He asked God for confirmation to make sure his small army could overtake the Philistines. When we humbly go to God to ask for confirmation of His will, we must be ready for his answer. Whether it is Yes, No or Not Yet, know when to move and do what it takes to accomplish our purpose.

CHAPTER 9:

Investing in yourself & embracing your purpose

In Chapter 8, We discussed the many blessings that can come from seeking and fulfilling God's purpose for us. I also discussed the challenges that may accompany you along the way. In this chapter I want to turn to the aspect of exactly *how* we can fulfill our God-given purpose.

How do we fulfill God's purpose? The basic principles are found in total surrender, obedience, and prayerful communication with God, humility, vigilance against the devil, steadfast faith, and perseverance. Doing all these things, will open doors for opportunities that will allow you expand and share your purpose in life. In this new life, you will accumulate blessings rather than collecting material things. These mini blessings will fill your life and there will be such an overflow of God's presence in your life that you can pour His love into others.

In addition to these general principles, it is also crucial that you invest spiritually in yourself and your mental health in order to fulfill your purpose in life. The day my Bishop said, "The measure of your faith determines your victory," something awakened in me in a positive way. I went into my prayer closet after church and asked God to build up my faith and obedience. I wanted my victories to reflect my Faith. I wanted God to show me the gifts He has given me, and how I could develop them to better serve Him.

My God-given talents are most likely different from yours. Individual gifts vary, but everyone *is* adorned a gift because God created everyone for a unique purpose. Understanding this, you have to resist the temptation to underestimate yourself and what God has for you this given moment. Do not settle for mediocrity, because God is not a mediocre God. We all have the responsibility to discover what our God-given talents are, and to develop those talents to their fullest potential in order to serve God.

When we underestimate ourselves, we underestimate God. When we question our worth, we are essentially questioning why God created us. It still perplexes me how some presume to think they know better than God and live by their own might! People so often fail to comprehend the magnitude of God's power and love. Let us remember that God is not bound by limitations of the mind and fear. God transcends space and time within their boundaries. With one word, the universe came into being and stars began to give off light. And according to the Bible, humans are the crown jewels of creation. We have to trust that God has great plans for us. I use to be one of those people who went to church every Sunday, was touched by the sermons yet failed to apply and trust completely in God's power. Let us hold on to the Word of God and truly believe that our God is powerful and able to prosper us.

Invest in your purpose

When you embrace the biblical truth of individual gifts you will see yourself in God's image, and as a reflection of God's love. This is the most liberating experience you'll ever encounter. With that, you can accomplish anything by faith. Knowing that before the foundation of the world were existed, God had you in mind and designed a unique plan for you. God has made you a steward of your own unique talents, and it is your responsibility to cultivate and use those talents for His will.

When you embrace your worth as a child of God, you claim your inheritance. Invest in your faith, by listening to sermons and reading the source of life "the Bible". Take the initiative and attend programs and workshops geared towards accomplishing your calling. As you invest in these courses, you'll begin to understand the broad picture of what God has designed for you and continue to pray for confirmation and clarity.

The first program I signed up for programs that helped develop new and existing women entrepreneurs understand the principles on how to run and operate kingdom business and make profit. I knew the program would equip with tools needed for my purpose. By no means did I have funding for it but God provided just in time. Seek out people and communities that will encourage and evaluate you to explore your spiritual gifts.

Identify your Spiritual Gifts

How are you currently exercising your God-given gifts?

Identifying your spiritual gifts is one of the most important things in life, because knowing your gifts will provide insight into how you can fulfill your God-given purpose. One day, my best friend enlightened me by dropping this gem as she said, "The two most important days in your life the day you are born and the day you discover your purpose." It resonated so much with me because I finally knew what it meant to have a calling. Knowing your purpose and spiritual gifts give give you a clear vision and confidence that you are anointed and ready.

According to Romans 12:6-8, these are the spiritual gifts God has given to man: Prophecy, Serving, Teaching, Encouraging, Giving, leadership, mercy, Word of Wisdom, Word of Knowledge, Faith, Healing, Miraculous Powers, Discerning, Speaking in Tongues, and interpreting Tongues.

Through prayer and stillness with God, you will be able to identify your spiritual gifts and understand how to use them. Prayer is an investment in your present and future. The spiritual gifts are not given to us to enjoy behind closed doors. No, God created and anointed me with these gifts to serve Him, to fellowship and edify each other. When you are given spiritual gifts, you are equipped with the responsibility to use them to live up to the expectation and in most cases God will expand your territory.

The second program I invested in empowered startup businesses and those who have a business idea but needed the resources and knowledge to execute. God will lead you to these courses as you do the work

God will guide you if you do the work

Investing in myself by taking these programs allowed me to prepare for the business aspect of where God was taking me. I truly believed God will position certain resources in your path to prepare you. these programs should be aligned solely with your calling and where God want to take you. Sometimes you may even feel ill prepared or unworthy of sharing your journey but know your purpose is to help others in someway shape or form.

Vulnerability is a strength

God can breathe new life into you and lead you to an existence focused on giving life to others. His power is infinite and beyond understanding, and I can go on and fill hundreds of pages talking about God's track record of rescuing His children from any circumstance. But I encourage you to explore the Bible on your own, and allow God to lead you to the passages that speak to your unique circumstance. You may be fearful of the unknown journeys ahead. You may wonder how you will ever find out what your gifts are. You may be unsure how to find a place in this world to exercise your gifts. Don't worry. In Him there will be answers to all your questions. Just take it one step at a time, and trust Him to reveal the answers to you in due time. You will find those answers as you read the Word of God and pray to Him. As you become closer and closer to the heart of God through knowing His Word and talking to Him, it will become easier to discern His will and find the answers you need.

One of the struggles you may encounter as you pursue God's purpose is vulnerability in sharing your story in order to help others. Don't shy away from sharing your testimony, it maybe what someone needs in that moment. In the beginning I refrained from sharing my story of heartbreak, pain and rejection but the blessing that came from it far outweigh the pain. There is a reason people need to hear your story of redemption, be the change others need. Be bold, courageous and walk in authority. God has different purposes for different people, and for me He may want you to help people heal and understand the process. Dear millennial woman, it is a privilege to be used by God, allow Him to demonstrate His faithfulness and power in your weakness. Instead of focusing on what people might think of your story, focus being truthful and letting God's light shine through your healing.

Investing in yourself in order to accomplish your purpose can take many forms, and taking courses is just one of them. Another way to invest in yourself is to cultivate relationships. No man is an island, and we are meant to grow in a community. We need to learn to care for other people and be supported by other people. As we cultivate relationships, we also learn to love people the way God loves us. We learn to minister to people and meet them where they are. All of these experiences will help clarify what our calling in life is. The more we understand people and their needs, the more we can see the holes that we can fill with our spiritual gifts.

LOVE the woman within you

Love the woman you're becoming through this process, slay the past, and invest in yourself spiritually, mentally and physically. Millennial woman, your journey is just beginning operate on God's timeline.

God will bless you in ways unimaginable making original plans pale in comparison. Sometimes we envisioned so little for ourselves watching those around us when our minds are not focused on God. But when we allow His presence to penetrate our soul, and embrace His plans, our perspective changes.

"We know how much God loves us, and we have put our trust in his love," 1 John 4:16 (NLT).

Growth doesn't stop with age

As children of God, we never stop growing in Christ. There is always something to be learned each new day, whether you're 10, 30, 50, 70, or 90 years old. Every day we wake up to a new opportunity to grow in Him and be used by Him. It is a lifelong adventure! Before, I woke up each time chasing after goals I set for myself, not knowing if I would ever attain them. But now I know for sure that I *will* achieve my life purposes—because those are purposes ordained by God and God's plan never falls through. For me it is reassuring to wake up every day in prayer, asking, "Lord, what do you have in store for me today? Whatever it is, I'm ready for the Spirit to lead and guide me into fulfilling your works today." There is liberation and peace in entrusting your life to a powerful and all-knowing God, who has only plans to prosper you.

As long as you seek guidance spiritually, your journey will never be alone, God will provide helpers and cause mentors and resources to invest in your purpose of serving Him and His people.

CHAPTER 10:
Renew your mindset and regain your happiness

Renewing your mind

Once you unveil your purpose, there is a renewal of the mind that takes place—your perspective changes, and you start realizing that being aligned with God brings joy. Joy gives you an internal peace and an external glow incomparable to anything else in life. It comes from having unshakable knowledge of your identity. in Christ, determined since before the foundations of the earth. There is joy in knowing clearly who you are and where you are going. This kind of joy can only come from God. None of the earthly possessions can generate this kind of profound and long-lasting joy.

Although the path to your joy and contentment may take longer, trust God knows best, every blessing is on His time line. Stray away from worldly things based on instant gratification and wanting things now just because the flesh needs it. We live in a world that wants things to happen instantly. Dear millennial woman, it is essential to know God takes time designing our destiny and some blessings take time. God is patient enough to work with us through this process in order to draw out our full potential. I encourage you to take time with the process to see the glory of God.

God is a provider

"For I am about to do something new. See, I have already begun! Do you not see it? I will make a pathway through the wilderness. I will create rivers in the dry wasteland." Isaiah 43:19

God will renew you in ways you never expected. Most of the time we fail to see God's vision because we are caught up in our own narrow vision of the future, and we tend to want to stay in control. Listen, Moses was convinced that as a stutterer there was no way he could be the leader of Israel. But what did God accomplish through him? The deliverance of the entire people of Israel! Moses even spoke before Pharaoh, the most powerful ruler on earth at that time. God gave Moses the eloquence he needed to accomplish God's purpose through Aaron. He will also breathe new life into you and give you what you need to accomplish your purpose.

Give yourself time for this process. Do not lean on your own understanding to rush your future. Do not rush ahead of God as Abraham did, when he conceived with Hagar. God's promise was intended for Sarah and Abraham to bear a son. Allow God to do his job. Our responsibility is to activate a relationship with God The timing may seem protracted, but nothing is delayed in God's timing. Be patient in the process of renewal, and humbly learn the tools you need to master in order to fulfill your purpose. This way, your mind will be renewed to reflect God's perspective. It will allow you to see yourself as God in the reflection of His love. Then, when people see that you have a healthy and vibrant self-perception, they will know that you are a mature and grounded woman, not influenced by the whims and trends of this world.

Are you feeding your purpose?

"Rejoice in our confident hope. Be patient in trouble, and keep on praying." Romans 12:12

The renewal of your mind requires you to remove all the clutter from your life so that you can focus on hearing God. There are so many distractions in our times that interrupt that stillness. These distractions can be people, addictions, depression, stress, or anything else that takes your mind away from God. We need to be responsible stewards of life and be careful with how we conduct ourselves, including who we associate ourselves with, what we watch on TV, what we eat, how we spend our time. The more responsible you become, the more God will entrust you joy with greater things.

God made a pathway through the wilderness and created rivers in the dry wasteland. With a renewed mind people may not recognize your spirit and that is fine as long as you're walking in purpose. Investing in yourself spiritually, mentally and physical is the only way to live in peace. Allow God breathe new life in you to help you overcome the fear of forgiving and letting go of past. Dear Millennial woman, I do not know what situation you're going through nor do I know God's purpose for you, but my hope is you seek Him long enough to find out for yourself. Do not allow society to define you. Whatever God has planned for you to accomplish, He will also renew you so that you are empowered to carry out the task. You will be surprised with how much God use you to manifest His glory!

Thank God for the closed doors. Know what you've been promised as millennial women and hold on in faith. For every love story God has ordained, He will uniquely package it and perfect all in His perfect timing. There is no need to seek after worldly validation. Be content with your current situation and actively seek to develop your God-given gifts as you await your blessings.

Be content in waiting

"Yet, I am confident I will see the LORD's goodness while I am here in the land of the living. Wait patiently for the LORD. Be brave and courageous. Yes, wait patiently for the LORD." Psalm 27:13

As you wait patiently on the Lord, learn to be joyful and content. A lot of times being joyful is a matter of choice. You can choose to be content with what God has given you and be joyful in God's guidance and plan. Or sulk for not being able to take control and make things happen your way. But there are times when it's not exactly a choice you can make. If you find yourself unable to be joyful, however you try, it may be time to seek God or professional help or spiritual counseling. Once you have received the appropriate treatment and have dealt with the underlying issues, joy really is within grasp. *"With joy you will draw water from the wells of salvation."* Isaiah 12:3

"Fearing people is a dangerous trap, but trusting the Lord means safety." Proverbs 29:25

The process of healing and renewal will have you learn to shift our focus away from the world and back to the Lord. If we are not vigilant, the world is full of temptations and traps that lure us into fear—fear of people, inadequacy, worthlessness, fear of failure...etc. We can be so fearful that we are paralyzed in life. But when you are renewed in Christ, you will be filled with boldness and authority. In the safety of a gracious God, we can freely pursue our purpose in life without being afraid of people's criticism or discouragement.

"For they loved human praise more than the praise from God." John 12:43

In the past there were times when the fear of man plagued my life because I wanted their praise more than Gods blessing. That caused a lot of roadblocks in my twenties. Many millennial women live this way and sometimes, the desire for validation from man tends to dictate your life decisions and steer us farther and farther away from where God wants to take us. That is why we suffer. When you become healed and renewed in Christ, you will learn to be in love with God first. You will learn to see His favor as superior to whatever compliments people can give you. From your secure position in God's arms, you will have a joy that cannot be taken away from you. Indeed, it is a joy for all eternity: *"You make known to me the path of life; in your presence there is fullness of joy; at your right hand are pleasures forevermore" (Psalm 16:11).*

Are You Satisfied? Or Just Existing?

In our old selves, we were restless, always pursuing the next thing that would validate our worth. When we achieved something, we became satisfied for a while before feeling the need to reach the next goal. The pattern of striving, instant gratification, and striving again, goes on and on without end. This kind of life cannot bring true satisfaction. All it is is temporary happiness, void of meaning.

For years I lived in that kind of pattern. I just...existed, going through the motions of the world with a 9 to 5 and no purpose to fill. There was no true joy to be found. Eventually, I realized it wasn't enough. I needed to actually *live*. I needed purpose and to stop looking for the next job and follow God. I needed to understand what true satisfaction was and how to attain it. The point is, no amount of money can bring you true happiness until you find peace in God's presence. Know that with him is where dreams come alive. Don't heat yourself out of peace and joy.

"Behold, I will bring to it health and healing, and I will heal them and reveal to them abundance of prosperity and security." Jeremiah 33:6

When you have been healed and renewed, this is what is available to you in Christ: an abundance of prosperity and security. There will be no more struggling and reaching. Only peace and eternal satisfaction.

Contentment and Joy

Just like the satisfaction the world offers us is drastically different from what God offers us, the happiness we can gain from the world is light years away from the true joy available in God. Happiness from the world leaves you hungry and in confusion. Paul describes contentment and joy with this passage.

"Not that I am speaking of being in need, for I have learned in whatever situation I am to be content. I know how to be brought low, and I know how to abound. In any and every circumstance, I have learned the secret of facing plenty and hunger, abundance and need." Philippians 4:11-12

Being content means knowing that there is more to life than earthly possessions. When your identity is firmly rooted in Christ, you can be content and joyful in any circumstance: plenty or poor, abundance or in need, you will be patient as God reveals His purpose to you and guides you to an abundant life. Being content in Christ means you are at peace with God's purpose for you and ready to be used by Him.

"And we are writing these things so that our joy may be complete." John 15:11

As you find pleasure in being content, your perspective will change. There will be no more comparison, and a need to find security, acceptance, or love from other people. The renewal will not happen overnight, nor is it easy. The different stages will require numerous baby steps in God's direction, and gradually you'll experienced increasing levels of joy and contentment. But the hard work really does pay off! With total surrender, God will grant you double portions of blessings in every aspect of your life. Everyday you'll relish in the sweetness of the joy and contentment in my life, marveled with peace. This joy, contentment, and peace is eternal if endure the process.

"Yet true gladness with contentment is itself great wealth. After all, we brought nothing with us when we came into this world and we can't take anything with us when we leave it." 1 Timothy 6:6

"A joyful heart is good medicine, but a crushed spirit dries up the bones." Proverbs 17:22

The Bible's definition of joy is not feeling good or upbeat all the time—Rather, joy is the assurance of knowing God is in control in every step you take. As your joy and contentment increases, you begin to bless others and make their joy complete. You can do so by exercising your gifts, helping others see their purpose in life, walking with those who are suffering or in the process of healing.

As I mentioned in a previous chapter, spiritual gifts are not given to us for our own enjoyment neither is your, it is meant to help others by sharing our testimony. Our rebirth and renewal comes with the responsibility of serving and edifying others with your renewed strength. The knowledge and wisdom you gain through God should be shared with others who have similar struggles. Nothing God has blessed you with is to be kept hidden. It is meant to be shared, nurtured, and passed down for generations.

God has created you to be a unique. He has special purposes for you to fulfill. Are you ready to be healed and renewed in order to fulfill those purposes? And are you ready to bless many others with your renewed mind and strength?

Reflection and Thanksgiving

As (you) continue to grow and embrace your experiences, stand in truth with no regrets because of God's grace. Be grateful that God allowed you to go through them in order to have this testimony to share with people and help them in their journey.

The process of healing and renewal will look slightly different in everyone's lives, because we are all made differently and have different pressure points in our lives. Learn to forgive yourself and see pass the roadblocks (failures) as part of the journey leading up to this moment. What you once considered a failure was preparing you for your purpose. God loves you enough bring you through difficulties in order to become stronger and wiser. The Bible says,

"Those who plant in tears will harvest with shouts of joy" (Psalm 126:5).

I have definitely lived this verse, and I am confident that you can, too. Dear millennial woman, my hope is that you grow in patience and increase your prayer life. Learn to be more like Hannah, who waited upon the Lord for years, all the while being patient and praising God. Cultivate patience and trust in Go and developed sensitivity to His voice. This will allow you to detect where You need to grow and humble you as you graciously minister to others.

"When I discovered your words, I devoured them. They are my joy and my heart's delight, for I bear your name, O LORD God of Heaven's Armies." Jeremiah 15:16

In my journey, I have also learned to depend on and stand on the word of God. In the Bible there is strength and comfort, and it is the Word of God that sustained me through many tearful nights. The Scriptures opened my eyes to see the spiritual reality of God's power and goodness, and my worth in Christ. Encourage yourself with the Word of God. Avail yourself of the power of prayer. Learn to praise Him no matter your circumstance—it is in doing so we learn to be content in God.

"Stay on the path that the LORD your God has commanded you to follow. Then you will live long and prosperous lives in the land you are about to enter and occupy." Duet 5:33 (NLT)

One reason why it is so important to stay on the Lord's path, is that God always reveals his promises. You never have to question God's intentions, On the other hand walking in the flesh leaves you wide open for plagues of doubt and confusion which leads to a path of destruction. The Word of God is life-giving, but the words of the world only tear you down. Chose to follow God's words to peace, or the carnal world will swallow you up and spit you out.

Speak life into yourself!

Proverbs 18:2 says, *"Death and life are in the power of tongue, and those who love it will eat its fruits."* Words are powerful. With words of persuasive authority, people have built up nations and torn down others. This is why we must renew our mind so that we desire to follow God's words, instead of believing the world's lies. As millennial Christian women, we need to speak life-giving words to bless other people. The power of life in the tongue must be used to breath life into others not to discourage people or destroy them.

You must use that power to empower and nurture others. With that, you also need the spirit of discernment to know when to distance yourselves from people who speak negatively into your life and devalue you. The Bible tells us that we'll be judged according to the words we speak: *"For by your words you will be justified, and by your words you will be condemned"* (Mathew 12:37). It is critical that we be renewed in our spirit, so that edifying, life-giving words pour out of our months.

The love of God must be present and a priority of life, otherwise you'll fall into sin. I experienced this vividly in my own experience. Do not placed your security and love in worldly pursuits, Instead, make God your priority and He'll show you the fruits of your labor. I hope that from this book, you have gained a clear understanding of God's promise. Set your path straight by aligning with God. I hope it is also clear that God will greet you with open arms, regardless of how much you think you've messed up.

Be thankful for the trials, growth, new adventures, and even the uncertainties ahead. All of these experiences big or small shape our character. They are meant to stretched us into committed servants for God. As you embark on your own journey of healing and renewal, you will also accumulate a long list of things you are thankful to God for. I am excited for your journey, and I wish I could hear about the success stories of all of my readers. I know that what God has done for me, He will do for *you* too!

Begin your journey with stillness and prayer. Pray for healing, guidance, clarity, and purpose. Heal from your mistakes, broken heart and people that hurt you. Slay the noises of the world and your fears. There is hard work ahead, but every bit of it will be worth it and God will never leave your side!

CONTACT INFORMATION

For more information about the author and booking opportunities, please
contact **amarenewllc@gmail.com** or
visit **www.prayhealslay.com**

Spiritual Counseling:

Contact the me or your membership-affiliated church to get connected to a local church.

Made in the USA
San Bernardino, CA
03 May 2017